The New
SOVIET
CONSTITUTION
of 1977

The New SOVIET CONSTITUTION of 1977

Analysis and Text

Analysis by

Robert Sharlet

Union College

JN
6515
A5
1977

KING'S COURT COMMUNICATIONS, INC.
BRUNSWICK, OHIO

SECOND PRINTING — AUGUST 1978

King's Court Communications, Inc.
Post Office Box 224
Brunswick, Ohio 44212
    Library of Congress
    Catalogue Card Number 77-95040

    ISBN: 0-89139-024-3

In Memory of My Mother
Evelyn Lillian Sharlet

"We are about to adopt the new Constitution on the eve of the 60th Anniversary of the Great October Socialist Revolution. This is not a mere coincidence in time of two major events in the life of our country. The connection between them goes much deeper. The new Constitution, one might say, epitomises the whole sixty years' development of the Soviet state. It is striking evidence of the fact that the ideas proclaimed by the October Revolution and Lenin's precepts are being successfully put into practice."

—Leonid Brezhnev
to the USSR Supreme Soviet
October 4, 1977

Preface

This book is intended to provide students of the Soviet, communist, and comparative political and legal systems with an analytical introduction to the new Soviet Constitution of 1977, a political and legal document of major importance to the understanding of the contemporary USSR. For this purpose, the book includes my essay "The New Soviet Constitution of 1977: Draft, Discussion, Revision, Ratification," followed by the official text of the new Soviet Constitution of 1977. In addition, a list of general textbooks on Soviet politics has been appended at the end of the book for students who may wish to inquire further about particular features of the Soviet system discussed in the essay or described in the Constitution.

An earlier version of this essay was published in *Problems of Communism,* XXVI, 5 (September-October 1977), pp. 1-24. For his editorial assistance on the original version, I would like to thank Peter Hauslohner, an associate editor of the journal. For the present volume, that essay has been revised, updated, and supplemented with a new section analyzing the amendments to the Draft Constitution and the final revision and ratification process.

The English translation of the 1977 Constitution is reprinted here by permission from the *Current Digest of the Soviet Press,* XXIX, 41 (November 9, 1977), pp. 1-13. The translator's italics and brackets have been retained to indicate where additions to, and deletions from the earlier draft version of the Constitution were made in the final text of the document.

R.S.
1978

Contents

DRAFT, DISCUSSION, REVISION, RATIFICATION

ANALYSIS BY ROBERT SHARLET

In 1977 — after nearly 20 years in the making — the Soviet Union finally promulgated its long-awaited new Constitution. With little advance warning, impending publication of the draft document was announced at a Central Committee plenary session in late May. But the significance of this event was at once overshadowed by the simultaneously announced ouster of Nikolay Podgornyy from the CPSU Politburo. Podgornyy's dramatic exit from the party leadership and his "request" for retirement from chairmanship of the Presidium of the USSR Supreme Soviet paved the way for General Secretary Leonid Brezhnev to be elected to the Soviet "presidency" at the regular Supreme Soviet session in mid-June.[1]

Thus, in the space of a few weeks, Brezhnev reached the summit of his political career. Having successfully engineered the fall of a reputedly major Politburo rival, he became the first CPSU leader to serve as not only de facto but also de jure head of state. In this new capacity, he immediately embarked on a major and well-publicized state visit to France, where his reception was marked by considerable ceremony. Yet while the General Secretary's new office attracted the most attention abroad, the proposed Constitution quickly occupied center stage at home. Indeed, the nationwide "public" discussion of the Draft during the summer and early fall followed by revision and ratification of the 1977 Constitution in October, took on the central role in the activities leading up to the celebration on November 7 of the 60th anniversary of the Bolshevik Revolution.[2]

The process of drafting a new Constitution was not a smooth one. The published Draft surfaced after nearly two decades of discussion and uncertainty — not just about its contents but about whether it would even appear at all. Entangled in the politics of destalinization, the passage of the new Soviet Constitution through the more open, factionalized, and conflict-ridden policymaking process of the post-Stalin era proved a complex undertaking, requiring numerous changes and compromises to accommodate the diverse interests involved in such a broad, overarching document.

The Path of Constitutional Reform

These circumstances contrast considerably with those surrounding the appearance of the "Stalin Constitution" some four decades before. A constitutional commission was appointed in 1935 and charged with replacing the constitution of 1924, which, after nearly a decade of social upheavals, no longer reflected the structure and content of the rapidly changing Soviet system. The commission produced a draft by mid-1936 and submitted it for nationwide discussion during the summer and fall. After mainly stylistic and semantic changes, it was ratified in late 1936, and December 5 has since been celebrated as "Constitution Day," invariably calling forth paeans of praise in the nation's media.[3]

The times then, of course, were very different. By the mid-1930's, Stalin had completed his "revolution from above," radically transforming the socioeconomic configuration of Soviet society in the process and, at the same time, ensuring his personal ascendancy over party and state. With collectivization behind him and heavy industrialization well under way, Stalin chose to consolidate these changes and stabilize the resulting status quo. Among other things this entailed reconstructing the legal system as a means of providing a formal framework for the planned, public economy, and of affording a larger measure of predictability to the individual citizen, who had just lived through a time of extraordinarily disruptive, indeed violent, social change. Toward this end, Soviet civil law, which had been rapidly "withering away" under the impact of radical Marxist jurisprudence, was gradually revived. A collective farm statute, legislating the peasant's rights to a personal garden plot, was enacted in 1935; and new, more conservative family legislation, designed to stabilize the family as a social unit, was passed in mid-1936. The new Constitution which followed served as Stalin's most public "signal" that the "revolution from above" was over and that "stabilization" was the new political and legal order of the day.[4]

The "Stalin Constitution" proclaimed that the Soviet Union had become "a socialist state of workers and peasants." It implied that the class war had ended, secured the peasant's garden plot in basic law, and constitutionally mandated the citizen's right to personal property. Although the "great purge" was reaching its crescendo at the same time, and while the new constitutional guarantees of personal security were being honored in the breach for millions of Soviet citizens, the personal economic rights granted under the "Stalin Constitution" did extend to the individual some greater degree of certainty in his daily life.[5]

After the dictator's death and the onset of destalinization, the rapid pace of reform and developmental change soon surpassed the Constitution's structural capacity to reflect it through the usual piecemeal process of amendment and revision. Efforts to draft a new Soviet Constitution formally began in 1962, but the removal of Nikita Khrushchev two years later understandably interrupted the process.[6] Brezhnev was elected Chairman of the Constitutional Commission in place of the deposed Khrushchev; thus the project was not abandoned. Yet, while the post-Khrushchev leadership thereby maintained a commitment to replace the supposedly long outdated "Stalin Constitution," progress on a new draft slowed appreciably.[7] Nor was this surprising, since previous Soviet constitutions had reflected each succeeding phase of Soviet political development, and since the Brezhnev regime in the latter half of the 1960's set about counterreforming many of Khrushchev's innovations while advancing new policies of its own. Another plausible reason for the delay in constitutional change was that the project presumably did not have the same priority for the pragmatic Brezhnev that it had for his more ideological predecessor. The 1936 Constitution was easily amendable; the more serious gaps could be filled by additional statutory legislation, and the major anachronisms superseded by new legislative principles and codes. Thus, the long established practice of incremental constitutional change could be continued while the post-Khrushchev leadership addressed itself to the more urgent problems of agriculture, the economy, and foreign policy.

In the late 1960's and early 1970's, however, several Western scholars learned in private talks with Soviet colleagues that the drafting process was under way once again.[8] The prospects for imminent constitutional change gradually gathered a modest momentum in the Soviet legal press and were stimulated from time to time by authoritative political hints. Speculation over the timing of the new Constitution was rife among Western specialists, although anticipation from all quarters mounted as the 25th CPSU Congress approached. The most popular scenario making the rounds among Western journalists and scholars at the time predicted that Brezhnev would crown his career with a new Constitution, to be presented at the Congress, which, presumably, would be Brezhnev's last in view of his age and deteriorating health. But the expected announcement failed to materialize, and Brezhnev confined himself to fresh promises on the subject in a few brief remarks at the end of his long opening-day Report. His statement that work on the constitution was going forward, although "without haste," was echoed subsequently in the legal press, but without elaboration or indication of any deadline for completion.[9] Then, without the usual advance clues, there came the abrupt announcement in May 1977 that the new Draft Constitution would soon be published for nationwide discussion.[10]

Continuity and Change

In keeping with Brezhnev's political style, the Constitution is a moderate, middle-of-the-road document, neither anti-Stalinist nor neo-Stalinist in its thrust, but rather a generally pragmatic statement of already existing practice and principle. Despite its association with the General Secretary's concurrent political triumphs, however, this document should not be regarded simply as a "Brezhnev Constitution." In the first place, as stressed in its Preamble, the 1977 Constitution displays much "continuity of ideas and principles" with the three previous constitutions.[11] For example, most of the articles dealing with property and the economy (Chapter 2 of the Constitution) and with the ordinary citizen's economic rights and duties (Chapter 7) date from the 1936 Constitution, in which they helped institutionalize and consolidate Stalin's "revolution from above." Moreover, Brezhnev himself made constitutional "continuity" a keynote in his plenum Report.[12]

Second, and of much greater importance, the 1977 Constitution codifies major social and political changes which extend beyond the scope of Brezhnev's leadership alone. In the most general sense, this is demonstrated by the fact that Soviet authorities describe it as the constitution of an advanced industrial society, one which, in Soviet parlance, has reached the stage of "developed socialism" (*razvitoy sotsializm*). In contrast, earlier constitutions were designed to serve a Soviet society at very different stages of revolutionary development or post-revolutionary consolidation.

More specifically, the new Constitution takes full account of the great volume of post-Stalin legislation that has affected nearly every branch and area of Soviet law. In fact, there are few points in the Constitution which have not been raised or institutionalized already in code law, statutory legislation, or the scholarly juridical commentary explicating the extensive post-Stalin legal reforms. For example, the environmental protection clauses (Arts. 18 and 67), the foreign policy section (Arts. 28-30), and the constitutional prescription (and pun) of a 41-hour maximum work week in Article 41 are all novel in comparison with the 1936 Constitution. But they break no new ground in terms of post-Stalin policy, practice, and legal development.[13]

In broader terms, the Constitution serves as a useful register of both the accomplishments and the limits of destalinization. In retrospect, it is clear that Khrushchev himself set out the boundaries of destalinization in his famous "secret speech" to the 20th Party Congress in 1956. Although he indicted Stalin for the "cult of personality" and its egregious consequences for the party and "socialist legality," Khrushchev also explicitly praised his predecessor for the latter's "great services to the party" in forging the socioeconomic foundations of the Soviet system, laid out in the course of the first Five-Year Plan.[14]

One major aspect of destalinization affirmed in the new document is the constitutionally enhanced status of the individual in relation to the state, especially in criminal proceedings (Arts. 151 and 160) but in civil matters as well (Art. 58).[15] No less important is the formally institutionalized "leading" role of the party (Art. 6), a change in constitutional form that culminates the party's renaissance following the end of Stalin's personal dictatorship. At the same time, the moderate tone and obvious compromises in the Constitution illustrate the consequences of post-Stalin leadership change, political factionalism, and interest group conflict.

The limits to change, however, are no less significant. Most important, the party has constructed in the new Constitution a political instrument for routinizing the governance process, but it has done so in such a manner as to leave sufficient ambiguity for a jurisprudence of political expediency to circumvent the system of "legality" (*zakonnost'*) when necessary. In fact, the party has merely "constitutionalized" the traditional dualism of law and extralegal coercion.[16] In this fundamental sense, the 1977 Constitution represents codification of the post-Stalin system as a party-led constitutional bureaucracy.

Still, a potentially important qualification should be added. During the course of the lengthy constitutional drafting process, a lively theoretical debate developed among Soviet legal scholars over the concept of "constitution" in Soviet jurisprudence. In essence, two schools of thought vied in the legal press over the seemingly "academic" question of whether to call Soviet public law "state law" (*gosudarstvennoye pravo*) or "constitutional law" (*konstitutsionnoye pravo*).[17] In fact, this debate held significant implications for the 1977 Constitution's draftsmen. "State law" refers to the traditional view which argues that the Soviet Constitution basically is intended to reflect the structure of state power prevailing in Soviet society. From this perspective, the Constitution, through the continuous process of amendment, performs little more than a codification function, recording and legitimating the changes in state structure as they occur.

The "constitutional law" school, which for years was in a decided minority within the Soviet legal profession, asserts that the traditional approach tends to reduce the Constitution to a mere sociopolitical mirror while neglecting its normative potential. In contrast, this side proposes that the Constitution be conceptualized as both a reflective *and* a programmatic instrument. The latter function would incorporate the Communist Party's ideological and policy goals into a more open-ended, future-oriented document. The "constitutionalists" also insist that their perspective would better facilitate the constitutional elaboration of the citizen's increased rights and duties, which have found legislative expression in the context of the changing post-Stalin relationship between state and individual.

The "constitutional" school seems to have prevailed[18] — at least to the extent that the 1977 Constitution includes greater programmatic content in comparison with the 1936 version. A further "constitutionalist" contribution may be the Constitution's greater emphasis on the sociopolitical, economic, and legal status of the Soviet citizen and the explicit correlation of the state's powers with its corresponding obligations to the citizen and vice versa.

To be sure, the party leadership intends to use the post-Stalin Constitution as a stable and orderly framework through which to govern the increasingly differentiated and specialized socioeconomic system, while at the same time reserving for itself the inherent power of dictatorship to bypass the "legal state" by resorting to *ad hoc*, extra-legal action when it thinks appropriate. Yet, in addition to providing a general legal policy that fixes the boundaries and functions of the social regulation process in higher law, the new Soviet Constitution itself contains the seeds of a major party metapolicy — that is, a set of goals and rules of behavior, given normative value and with system-wide and not merely legal ramifications.[19]

A Soviet "Systems" Approach

As expressed by Soviet political and legal commentators, a major purpose of the new Soviet Constitution is to reflect the infrastructure of the Soviet system now, after 60 years of development. In particular, this means recording in constitutional language the most important and enduring political, legal, socioeconomic, and doctrinal changes since promulgation of the 1936 Constitution, and especially following Stalin's death. In this connection, the more dynamic, "systems" approach to sociopolitical structure that is contained in Part I of the Constitution (Arts. 1-32) stands in decided contrast to the static, state-society formula of its predecessor.

Western-style "systems analysis" has come into vogue in the Soviet social sciences in recent years, although its reception in jurisprudence is still in its formative stage. In its legal context, the "systems" approach stems from post-Khrushchevian recognition of the distinction between the state (*gosudarstvo*) and the political system (*politicheskaya organizatsiya sovetskogo obshchestvo*).[20]

The Constitution's description of the whole Soviet system therefore delineates a dominant political system (Chapter 1), together with economic and social subsystems (Chapters 2 and 3). This framework implies a possible concession of at least some developmental autonomy for social and economic patterns in Soviet society. And it may suggest a perceptible change in stress, from a political system which is essentially transformist, to one which is more explicitly regulative.[21] The introduction of a new article which appears to advance the notion of "political culture" (Art. 9) stands in support of this interpretation.[22] Moreover, Chapter 4, which describes the functions of the Soviet system in the international environment (foreign policy), and Chapter 5, which describes the functions of defending the Soviet system from possible threats in the international environment, suggest extension of the "systems" model to a global scale.

One particularly notable feature of the post-Stalin "political system" is the doctrinal evolution from the "dictatorship of the proletariat" to "the state of all the people." Although Soviet jurists have failed to conceptualize this notion clearly since it first emerged under Khrushchev, the "state of the whole people," to a large extent, remains today — as earlier — a political metaphor signaling the leadership's interest in greater participation in the implementation of the party's policies by both mass organizations (Art. 7) and the public in general (Art. 5).[23] These participatory declamations are in turn operationalized in Articles 113 and 114, which provide, respectively, for legislative initiative by mass organizations and for general discussion of draft legislation by the public as a whole. With regard to both, however, the new Constitution merely confirms existing practice.

Chapter 1 also includes a clause on the legal subsystem, a reference which points to another of the major changes in the post-Stalin period. The 1936 Constitution included a statement of the citizen's duty to obey the law,[24] but the present document requires both the citizen (Arts. 59 and 65) and the state (Arts. 4 and 57) to observe the requirements of "socialist legality." Of course, the state's obligation to observe the law gives first priority to its function of protecting "law and order," a key slogan of the Brezhnev period.[25]

Finally, Article 6 in Chapter 1 makes explicit a party-dominant political system. The Communist Party, which was mentioned twice in the 1936 Constitution and only in connection with the rights of mass organizations,[26] has been institutionalized in the new Constitution as "the leading and directing force of Soviet society, the nucleus of its political system" — finally in accord with its actual role during the past decades of Soviet history. Since the Preamble declares that the Soviet system will strive to build communism in the future, the party's role is described in the more functional terms of serving as the guiding source for the domestic and foreign policy of the USSR.

The chapter on the economy describes the same infrastructure of public and personal economy set forth in the 1936 Constitution but also consolidates those structural changes associated with post-Stalin economic development.[27] Thus, Article 9 of the 1936 Constitution permitted the "small-scale private economy" of individual peasants and handicraftsmen; the corresponding Article 17 of the 1977 Constitution allows "individual labor activity" (*individualnaya trudovaya deyatel'nost'*) in the delivery of "consumer services for the population."[28] Trade union property has been added as a type of "socialist property" (Art. 10). This, of course, had been its de facto status for many years, a situation recognized formally in the 1961 Fundamental Principles of Civil Legislation. The planning clause (Art. 16) incorporates some of the features of "Libermanism" and the 1965 economic reforms with its reference to the "economic independence and initiative of enterprises, associations, and other organizations" and its explicit bow to the importance of profits, costs, and *khozraschët* (economic accountability). Article 18 declares the state's commitment to the protection and rational utilization of the environment, an injunction of both reflective and programmatic dimensions.

More purely programmatic is the consumption and labor productivity clause (Art. 15), which earmarks social production (*obshchestvennoye proizvodstvo*) for the satisfaction of people's wants and needs and charges the state with the task of raising labor productivity in order to fulfill this commitment. The prominence accorded consumer needs in Articles 14 and 15 of the Constitution constitutes a marked departure from the corresponding passage in the "Stalin Constitution" which placed relatively greater stress on economic growth.[29] Both the socialist emulation or competition technique, "inspired" by Stakhanov in the 1930's, and the more recently launched "scientific-technological revolution" are invoked in quest of higher labor productivity. In view of the questionable effectiveness of the former technique and widespread doubts regarding Soviet capacity to stimulate and manage innovation, Article 15 is likely to remain more programmatic than "reflective" for some time.[30]

Finally, the 1936 exhortation to work has been softened somewhat in the new Constitution (Art. 14) but nonetheless ends on a phrase which maintains the spirit of the anti-parasite legislation: *"socially useful* labor and its results shall determine the status of a person in society" (italics added).[31] This impression is strengthened in the more exhortative "rights and duties" section (Art. 60), in which "conscientious labor in one's chosen field of socially useful activity" is described as both a duty and a "matter of honor."

The chapter on the social subsystem consists largely of a set of programmatic directional signs on the road to communism, as Brezhnev acknowledged in his plenum Report. Included are commitments to the enhancement of social homogeneity (Art. 19), the eventual abolition of manual labor through mechanization (Art. 21), and the development of consumer services (Art. 24) — all in connection with the long-standing commitment to encourage development of the "new man" (Art. 20). These social articles in the 1977 Constitution give rise to a sense of *déjà vu* — the rhetoric is reminiscent of Khrushchev's 1961 Party Program, minus the detail and accompanying timetable for the realization of specified goals.[32]

The short chapters on foreign policy and defense contain a mix of reflective and programmatic elements but basically proceed from recognition of the fact that the Soviet Union has emerged as a superpower. There is here, too, a degree of continuity with the 1961 Party Program, particularly in the clauses on peaceful coexistence (Art. 28) and socialist (read "proletarian") internationalism (Art. 30).[33] Absent, in comparison with the earlier documents, are the repeated references to world capitalism and imperialism and the spirit of competition with the West. Article 29 essentially incorporates the Helsinki principles. At the same time, the socialist internationalism clause has been written broadly enough to accommodate both the Brezhnev doctrine and Soviet leadership of the Council for Mutual Economic Assistance (CMEA).[34] The defense clauses offer a straightforward elaboration of the State's defense function that was described in the 1936 Constitution.[35] In addition, the state's defense functions and foreign policy objectives have been supplemented by the citizen's military obligation (Art. 63), the more diffuse duty "to safeguard the interests of the Soviet state and to help strengthen its might and prestige" (Art. 62), and a still vaguer "internationalist duty" (Art. 69).

The Citizen and the State

The second main purpose of the new Constitution is to define the relationship between the state and the individual. This relationship can be divided, for analytic purposes, into the citizen's economic, civil, and participation rights and duties.

Economic rights. The economic rights need only brief review, since they are the same rights as those of the 1936 Constitution, albeit with a few additions and amplifications.[36] A constitutional guarantee of housing (Art. 44) and the right to use the achievements of culture (Art. 46) have been added, while the 1936 Article on economic security has been expanded and divided in the 1977 Constitution into two articles on health protection (Art. 42) and old age maintenance (Art. 43). The right to work also has been enlarged to include the freedom to choose one's profession, occupation, or employment, provided the choice is consistent with society's needs (Art. 40), a constitutional "right" made possible by the higher level of economic development and general affluence of Soviet society today as compared with life in the mid-1930's. Indeed, while many of the economic rights were programmatic when first included in the "Stalin Constitution," they are now, for the most part, simply reflective of a highly developed welfare state.[37]

At the same time, the economic rights of the Soviet citizen are balanced by a basic economic "duty," also carried over from the 1936 Constitution. In this connection, the citizen's obligation to protect socialist property has been reaffirmed, although in destalinized form — that is, public property is no longer described as "sacred and inviolable," and persons who commit property crimes are no longer castigated as "enemies of the people." The property protection clause is already amply supported in the criminal codes of the various union republics. Yet, in view of the extent of economic crime and the scale of the "second economy" or "parallel market," it would seem fair to predict that countless Soviet citizens, from factory workers to enterprise directors, will continue to disregard this constitutional injunction.[38]

Civil liberties. The civil rights clauses of the new Constitution, which should be judged together with the sections on the courts (Chapter 20) and the Procuracy or prosecutor's office (Chapter 21), reveal much more about the citizen's status vis-à-vis state and provide further evidence for assessing the current scope and limits of destalinization. Most important, the basic civil rights continue to be limited by the standard caveat that the rights of speech, press, association, assembly, public meetings, and demonstration are guaranteed to the citizen only in conformity with "the people's interests and for the purpose of strengthening" and developing the socialist system (Arts. 50-51).[39] The same preference for the social over the individual interest also limits the new civil right of "freedom of scientific, technical, and artistic creation" (Art. 47). In fact, the new Constitution has two additional paragraphs that further emphasize the social limits on the citizen's right to exercise his economic rights and his civil liberties. In the article introducing Chapter 7, on the "Basic Rights, Liberties, and Duties of USSR Citizens," Soviet citizens first are granted the "whole range of social, economic, political and personal rights and liberties" which follow — but under the condition of the closing injunction which points out that the "exercise of rights and liberties by citizens must not injure the interests of society and the state or the rights of other citizens" (Art. 39). The predominence of the prevailing social interests is reinforced in the "duty to obey" clause (Art. 59). The spirit and some of the language of this clause incorporate most of the antecedent article from the 1936 Constitution,[40] although with an added phrase stressing the nexus between citizens' rights and their social obligations: "the exercise of rights and liberties is inseparable from the performance by citizens of their duties." Again, as with much of the Constitution's content, this concept of linkage does not represent an innovation in Soviet law. Moreover, it is relevant to all of the citizen's rights and obligations and is not addressed exclusively to the criminal justice process.[41]

Turning now to the position of the individual in the criminal justice system, we find that the most significant aspects of post-Stalin legislation on criminal law and procedure also have been incorporated into the new Constitution. From arrest through appeal, the position of the individual in the Soviet criminal justice process has been considerably strengthened since enactment of the all-union Fundamental Principles of Criminal Procedural Legislation in 1958.[42] A Soviet "due process" in *ordinary* (nonpolitical) criminal cases has developed and survived leadership turnover and the vicissitudes of Soviet politics.[43] For the vast majority of individual citizens, this may have been the most important and durable accomplishment of destalinization.

Much of this change, of course, arose from post-Stalin reaction to the conditions of official lawlessness and terror that prevailed at the time of the adoption of the 1936 Constitution and that continued, though significantly reduced in scale, up to and even after Stalin's death in 1953. Although the current personal inviolability clause (Art. 54) resembles its 1936 antecedent, the injunction against arrests without either court order or approval of a procurator is now grounded in the operative legislation and codes on criminal procedure as well as in actual post-Stalin Soviet practice.[44] After the arrest, contemporary Soviet justice is, in fact, "administered solely by the courts" (Art. 151). The judiciary clause in the new Constitution is far more explicit in this respect than its predecessor and is firmly based on the Fundamental Principles of Legislation on the Court System of 1958. At the same time, neither the current clause nor the Fundamentals mention the existence of "special courts" which were acknowledged in the 1936 Constitution and which still exist.[45]

Once in court, the contemporary Soviet defendant, in theory and for the most part in practice, enjoys equality "before the law and the court" (Art. 156). In practical terms, the class approach to justice, characteristic of revolutionary Marxist legal theory, was generally abandoned in the late 1930's.[46] Still, it is doubtful that all Soviet citizens do, in fact, enjoy equal standing before the court "regardless of their social" or "official status," for in most legal systems, there often is an unacknowledged differential of treatment based on status, however it may be measured in a particular society.

The citizen's right to defense has also been strengthened in the new Constitution in accordance with previous legislative development. The 1936 Constitution contained a "right to defense" clause, the language of which is nearly the same as that of the current clause (Art. 158). But the right to defense is now supported by constitutional recognition of the collegia of defense attorneys and by the right of mass organizations to assign a "social defender" to a case in support of one of its members (Arts. 161 and 162).[47] To be sure, the defense bar has existed for a long time, and the institution of citizen defenders is rooted in the earliest days of Soviet legal history.[48] At the same time, the regime evidently has chosen to install these well-known institutions in the new Constitution as reaffirmation of the post-Stalin commitment to the Soviet version of due process. In this context, the "open court" clause (Art. 157), a carry-over from the Stalin Constitution, is now more meaningful and less frequently violated.[49]

The judiciary's constitutional monopoly over the administration of justice is explicitly reinforced in a clause that reflects post-Stalin dissolution of the notorious "special boards."[50] The constitutional declaration that "no one can be adjudged guilty of committing a crime and subjected to criminal punishment other than by the verdict of a court" and in accordance with law (Art. 160) is both a reminder of and a response to the extralegal traditions of Stalinism as well as one of several "signals" in the current document that there will be no return to what Brezhnev himself called in his

May 1977 plenum Report "the illegal repressions" that "darkened" the years following ratification of the 1936 Constitution.[51] Although the clause assuring judicial independence (Art. 155) still is liable to the party's contravention, there have been some indications, if difficult to document, that direct party interference in the work of the judiciary has abated since the Stalin years.[52] On the other hand, the individual's relationship to the state also has been at least somewhat clarified following destalinization of the Procuracy in 1955. Article 164 reflects in constitutional law the Procuracy's fully restored responsibility for overseeing compliance with the law — by institutions, organizations, officials, and ordinary citizens — and thus underscores the leadership's concern for administrative legality as part of a long-range effort to raise the public's legal consciousness and build a viable "legal culture" through which the party can insure that both the state and the individual observe the laws which express the party's policies.[53]

Collectively, these constitutional clauses appear to codify a significant stabilization in contemporary legislation and legal practice of the relationship between the individual and the state in Soviet society, particularly in the criminal justice process. Although many of Khrushchev's reforms have been repealed by the Brezhnev leadership, the policy and legislative commitment to "due process" for the criminal defendant has been maintained and even strengthened to some extent through the development of a body of "case law."[54]

With respect to the tiny minority of activist dissidents, however, both the personal security clauses and the formal rights accorded criminal defendants have been sorely abused by the regime, especially since the Sinyavskiy-

Daniel' trial in early 1966.[55] In the endless stream of dissident cases reported in *samizdat,* there have been numerous recorded violations of the inviolability of the home (Art. 55) and of the confidentiality of correspondence and telephone conversations (Art. 56). In recent years, incidents of intimidation, mugging, physical assault, and, in a few instances, death under mysterious circumstances — all believed to have been provoked or even perpetrated by KGB personnel in mufti — indicate that for dissidents the right to legal protection against threats against life and health, property and personal freedom and "honor and dignity" (Art. 57) is, for all practical purposes, a dead letter. If, as is often the case, the bureaucratic harassment and administrative actions directed against dissidents have led to criminal prosecution for either a political offense or an ordinary crime, the dissident defendant routinely finds his due process rights violated both in the preliminary investigation and during the subsequent trial. In fact, the constitutional due process clauses in the present document are frequently inverted to the disadvantage of the dissenter. Instead of executing his responsibility to legally prevent the official capriciousness experienced by dissidents (Art. 164), the procurator usually shares complicity. Rather than benefit from a strengthened right to defense (Arts. 158 and 161), the dissident's right to choose a defense counsel generally is subject to KGB interference and is frequently abridged. Finally, instead of enjoying equality before the law and the court (Art. 156), the dissident is classified as a "political case" and subjected systematically to a pattern of discrimination by the legal personnel formally involved and by the party and KGB officials who may discreetly direct the administration of political justice from behind the scenes. In effect, as Harold Berman has aptly pointed out, in political cases "socialist legality" breaks down into its constituent parts — socialism versus legality.[56]

The dissidents' response to the regime's political justice has been to put up a "legalist" defense, confronting the judges and prosecutors in an orderly fashion with a detailed and documented account of the violations of their due process rights.[57] In their "pretrial motions," their traditional "final word" to the court, and in the post-incarceration protests, dissidents caught up in criminal process and their supporters "replay" the law to their persecutors, citing the appropriate code articles, fundamental principles, and even constitutional clauses which the legal cadres and their mentors have violated. The legalist defense has not won any cases for dissenters. But, in using it, political defendants have succeeded repeatedly in indicting the regime and putting it "on trial" in the court of Western public opinion.

It is doubtful that the new Constitution's strengthened emphasis on the "public interest" will discourage significantly the "legalist" defense. The injunction against injuring one's fellow citizens and the society in the exercise of one's rights (Art. 39) and the "rights and duties" clause (Art. 59) are neither specially designed for dissidents nor exclusively relevant to criminal law. At best, these additional caveats merely reinforce the constitutional legitimacy of bringing political prosecutions against dissidents who have chosen to exercise their civil rights in contradiction to the officially defined social and political interests (Arts. 50 and 51). Still, assuming that the dissident or even an ordinary Soviet citizen failed to perform his duties and damaged the social interest (Arts. 59 and 39), there is nevertheless no constitutional mandate in either clause for denying that person the rights of personal security and due process that are incorporated into existing Soviet law on criminal procedure. That is, commission of a political offense does not waive an individual's right to due process as provided under the new Soviet Constitution. Yet what the regime does in practice in such cases is another matter. The legalist defense, focusing as it does on procedural violations, may be expected to continue in the future, with similar outcomes for both the dissidents and the regime's image abroad.

Participatory rights. The Soviet citizen's economic rights and civil liberties have been supplemented in the new Constitution by an increased emphasis on his participatory rights. In theory, this is a result of the transition from a proletarian dictatorship to a "state of all the people" (Art. 1). In structural terms, a greater scope and opportunity for citizen involvement in public life is outlined in the political and economic chapters of the Constitution reviewed above. The individual's specific participatory rights may be viewed as giving practical meaning to this enlargement of participatory space in the Soviet system. In general, the participatory rights are to be exercised mainly in the broad process of *policy implementation,* while the opportunity for greater citizen input into the *policymaking* process, as presented in the new Constitution, is confined at most to the arena of local government.

Thus, the new Constitution guarantees to the citizen the general right of public participation (Art. 48); the right to submit proposals and to criticize with impunity the performance of governmental agencies (Art. 49); the right to lodge complaints against public officials and, in some cases, to seek judicial remedy (Art. 58); and the right to sue government agencies and public officials for tort liability incurred by illegal actions causing the citizen-plaintiff damage (Art. 58).[58] In regard to the citizens' slightly increased opportunities for participating in local policy-making, Chapters 14 and 19 of the Constitution codify those post-Stalin changes in state law (*gosudarstvennoye pravo*) associated with the growth of the responsibilities of local soviets and of the powers of their deputies. In the spirit of the "all-people's state," the soviets of "working people's deputies" have been renamed soviets of "people's deputies" (Art. 89). And, consistent with the increased interest in citizen participation which began under Khrushchev and continues under Brezhnev, the new Draft Constitution was published in June 1977 for nationwide public discussion, as stipulated in its discussion clauses (Arts. 5 and 114).

Participation and Public Discussion

At midpoint in the nationwide public discussion, it was clear that the Draft Constitution was headed for ratification. Before the Draft had even been published, Brezhnev in his address to the May plenum referred to the document several times in a way which seemed to forecast ratification sometime in the fall of 1977. He considered in detail some of the problems involved in "implementation of the new Constitution," and he ended his Report on the reassuring note that "the adoption of the new USSR Constitution will be an important milestone in the country's political history."[59] Brezhnev's confidence about the prospects for ratification soon was echoed in lead editorials and the speeches of senior party leaders at meetings of major party organizations and at sessions of the union republic supreme soviets.[60] In a published interview with a Japanese correspondent several days after the public discussion began, Brezhnev again stressed the importance he attached to ratification, remarking that the "adoption of the new Constitution" would have great significance not only at home but abroad as well.[61]

With ratification thus a foregone conclusion, Brezhnev and the party leadership set the stage for a carefully planned, well orchestrated public "discussion" of the Draft during the summer and early fall of 1977. Enjoined by Brezhnev to take the lead in drawing "the mass of the working people and representatives of all strata of the population" into discussion and to use the occasion for "the further invigoration of all social life in the country,"[62] subordinate party leaders returned to their constituencies and made organization and leadership of the discussion a matter of highest priority for all party cadres under their jurisdiction.[63] Shortly after the Draft was published, a *Pravda* editorial appropriately characterized the discussion as an "exchange of opinion on the basic questions of the development of our society and state."[64] According to well-informed sources, special arrangements were made at every level of the Soviet system for recording the subsequent comments and suggestions, and for forwarding them to the Constitutional Commission for consideration.[65]

Specifically, every party organization, state institution, social organization, etc., was expected to discuss the Draft Constitution and forward its statement and/or proposals for amendment through the appropriate channels to the newly established Secretariat of the USSR Constitutional Commission (the Institute of State and Law of the USSR

Academy of Sciences reportedly played a key role in the work of the Secretariat). This Commission, together with its Editorial Subcommittee, was assigned the tasks of evaluating the amendments proposed in the course of the nationwide discussion and finalizing the Draft for the fall ratification session of the USSR Supreme Soviet.

In addition, prominent scholars, including several jurists, published in the leading newspapers lengthy individual articles presenting what appeared to be their personal views on the Draft Constitution. Evidently, many of those articles, especially those which appeared in June and July, had been written earlier, their authors having received advance copies of the Draft Constitution for this express purpose in the spring prior to the document's publication.

All commentary, both internal and published, was evaluated in generalized form by the Constitutional Commission in the process of revising the published Draft for final ratification in the fall of 1977. Toward this end, the Presidium of the USSR Supreme Soviet renewed the Commission in April 1977 by adding 21 new members to replace the 43 members who had "left" the Commission since its last reorganization in 1966, as a result of death, demotion, retirement, or failure to gain reelection as a Supreme Soviet Deputy. The April additions increased the size of the Commission to its 1966 strength of 75 members, among them various Politburo members, Central Committee secretaries, republic party first secretaries and premiers, officials of all-union state and public organizations, prominent individuals, and the leading legal officials (including Procurator-General R.A. Rudenko, Chairman of the USSR Supreme Court, Judge L.N. Smirnov, and USSR Minister of Justice V.I. Terebilov).[66]

Each member apparently was expected to represent his particular regional or institutional interests in the politics of revision and ratification.

While an analogous "public" discussion preceded ratification of the 1936 Constitution, extensive public "commentary" on various legislative proposals has become, since Stalin's death, a much more common method of involving the average citizen in public affairs. In general, this involvement is circumstantial and very limited — usually to no more than suggesting changes in tone, wording, or emphasis in a given piece of legislation, for which the basic framework already has been set by party authorities. Public discussion has thus become an oft-used leadership technique for mobilizing the population and encouraging citizen participation in policy *implementation,* while the party uses the occasion for a mass political socialization campaign at the same time.[67]

The 1977 constitutional discussion stood apart from previous discussions of legal reform, at least in terms of its scope and duration. But it marks no obvious watershed in either the extent of public political participation or in the quality of regime-society relations. It was extremely doubtful that the public discussion would result in significant changes in the Constitution before its ratification. At most, a number of major and minor semantic revisions and shifts in stress were anticipated, although attempting to link such changes with the public discussion was problematic at best in many instances. It is useful to keep in mind that the proposals or criticisms that appeared in the Soviet media, passed through several cautious and purposive "filters" and, therefore, reflected the inclinations and political sensitivities of editors, censors, and various party authorities, in addition to those of the given authors.

At the same time, it was almost surely the case that within general guidelines laid down by the central party leadership, editors and local government and party officials exercised a substantial amount of discretion in deciding which views were to be published. It also seems clear that the scope of what is considered permissible for public discussion in the Soviet press has grown enormously since Stalin's death, a development to which the 1977 constitutional discussion gave eloquent testimony. To be sure, commentary on certain issues remained proscribed. Thus, even passing remarks on the Draft articles concerning either the party's role or Soviet foreign policy were exceedingly rare in the discussion published in the general press. On the other hand, the discussion brought forth a remarkable variety of proposals on a wide range of concerns. In a narrow sense, the discussion afforded to individuals and groups an opportunity for self-advertisement and the promotion of group or institutional interests which might be advantaged by some constitutional modification. The discussion also served, however, as a forum for individuals who were more interested in the Constitution itself and certain of its provisions. This second category of commentators seemed to take rather seriously the normative potential of the Constitution, increasingly emphasized by Soviet legal scholars.

In general, then, the discussion of the 1977 Constitution represented an important indicator, in two major respects. First, the whole of the discussion for the most part delineated the boundaries of what the party leadership regards as legitimate for public consumption and consideration. Second, those particular issues which were raised indicate in which aspects of Soviet social, economic, and political life the party hopes to stimulate the public's interest, as well as those issues on which the party is willing to tolerate the public's comments and suggestions. This is the overarching context in the light of which the published discussion should be appraised.

In its opening weeks, this discussion was largely ceremonial in nature and produced little of substance. Major party organizations contributed laudatory statements to the pages of *Pravda* set aside for the discussion; *Izvestiya's* special page was used to accommodate the enthusiastic declarations of different union republic supreme soviets and their presidia. In the same vein, lengthy articles by major party and government figures appeared in both newspapers during June, primarily offering a recitation of various social and economic achievements within their signatories' jurisdictions.[68] At this stage of the discussion, numerous photos displaying the public's "enthusiasm" for the new document appeared throughout the press. And daily the major newspapers carried a page reserved for the nationwide discussion, which typically contained survey articles by correspondents reporting first impressions of ordinary citizens, a supportive statement by a worker and deputy to a local soviet, and often a more lengthy, obviously prepared essay by a scholar on a general theme of the Constitution. Occasionally, brief letters from average citizens were also included.

By the end of June, the discussion had mushroomed into a great volume of citizen activity. *Izvestiya,* for example, reported that it had received over two and a half million letters on the Draft, while the municipal party organization in Kiev announced that exactly 41,787 groups were discussing the Constitution in that city alone.[69] Meanwhile, below the surface of published comment more substantive consideration of the Draft already was taking place in every institution and organization throughout the nation. These aggregated comments, suggestions, and recommendations on different constitutional articles began to flow upward through the various hierarchies and, via specially established channels, to the Constitutional Commission in Moscow. Since only a small fraction of such statements could possibly be published or broadcast, the greater part of both the ceremonial and substantive discussions inevitably took place behind the scenes and out of the public's view.

Beginning in July, however, the published commentary took on a decidedly more substantive tone. A recurring pattern of issues, reflecting themes of the leadership, group interests, and individual concerns, began to emerge in the national and regional press. Basically, the nationwide discussion of the Draft seems to have revolved around three sets of issues — what I will call sociopolitical, socialist legality, and "motherhood" issues. Of course, this did not prevent publication of a diverse range of individual concerns: the citizen from Sverdlovsk who suggested adding to the personal property clause (Art. 13) explicit mention of an individual's right to own a car; or the pro-women's liberation letter which advocated that a phrase promising "equal pay for equal work" be given a place in the document (Art. 35).[70] One "old-timer," a member of the party since 1919 and a veteran of the discussion of the 1936 Constitution, simply expressed his pleasure at again having the opportunity to take part in such a great undertaking.[71] But for the most part these were isolated comments, tangential to the main lines of the discussion.

Worker discipline and productivity and socioeconomic and political participation were the "sociopolitical" issues that generated the greatest volume of attention — from party organizations, government agencies, managers, workers, and the average citizen. Two "socialist legality" issues — "law and order" and civil liberties — stimulated somewhat less voluminous but much sharper, more intense comment. Finally, numerous letters in support of environmental protection and the promotion of science appeared. No one, of course, explicitly opposed either of these, hence the label "motherhood issues."[72] Although these particular communications were marked by greater spontaneity, they were also notably less intense. If, in fact, there were *ad hoc* "lobbies" operating from below in the course of any part of the discussion, they would appear to have been the diffuse coalitions of specialists and concerned citizens that mobilized in response to these two concerns.

Some of the issues, both within and between categories, seemed to be complementary. A stress on "law and order" dovetailed nicely with support for public participation in peer justice institutions. Between other issues, however, there was natural, and not merely implicit, conflict. Such appeared to be the relationship between the numerous and aggressive "law and order" proposals and the fewer, though more articulate, propositions for strengthened civil liberties. Finally, some of the pro-science suggestions were relevant to production questions. In contrast, advocates of environmentalism seemed to stand alone, neither antagonistic to nor supportive of the other, basic issues in the discussion.

Sociopolitical Issues

At the heart of the "work issue" was the across-the-board concern over the need for improved labor discipline. Focused primarily on the labor discipline clause (Art. 60) and, to a lesser extent, on related ones (Arts. 14 and 40), numerous articles and letters called for recasting this theme with stronger language, greater emphasis, and, sometimes, the assistance of coercive remedies. Brezhnev touched on the general problem at the May plenum, and both *Pravda* and *Komsomol'skaya pravda* cued the issue in lead editorials specifically on Article 60.[73] While the public commentary included advice such as a factory *kollektiv's* suggestion of awarding more medals for good work and the woman engineer's argument that the Constitution must emphasize the correlation between marriage and a positive attitude toward work,[74] the mainstream of the discussion divided between those who recommended writing more moral stimuli into the pertinent articles (usually Art. 60) and those who favored adding more practical language — for example, the Lithuanian engineer who stressed the importance of mechanization and increased worker education "in the struggle to raise the effectiveness of production and the quality of work."[75] In general, most workers' comments inclined toward the moral approach, whereas management personnel seemed more likely to agree with the engineer's emphasis.

At the same time, a number of letter writers proposed a more coercive approach to the problem. One Moscow factory worker favored holding those who violate labor or production discipline "morally and materially responsible before society." In more specific terms, various engineers and skilled workers advocated adding to Article 60 the language of legal sanction. And several writers from the Ukrainian, Lithuanian, Kazakh, and Kirgiz Republics explicitly recommended including the letter and spirit of the extant anti-parasite legislation.[76]

In comparison with the "work" issue, the theme of socioeconomic and political participation evoked a much broader spectrum of interests. Concerns ranged from enhancing the individual's participatory rights of making suggestions (Art. 49) and filing complaints (Art. 58) to expanding institutional discretion in correspondence with responsibilities — of enterprises in economic decision-making (Art. 16) and of local soviets with respect to local socioeconomic development (Art. 146).

Institutional participation attracted the attention of middle-level elite members in particular. Both the Irkutsk Regional Party Committee and a Moscow factory manager, for example, offered nearly identical recommendations that supplementary wording be added to Article 16 to ensure that ministries be held accountable for their economic decisions and that they comply with existing legislation permitting greater initiative on the part of the enterprise.[77] (In somewhat related fashion, several letters from workers indicated interest in strengthening the section on worker participation in enterprise management,* although actual suggestions consisted of minor semantic revisions which seemingly would expand the scope of such participation only slightly.[78])

The status of local soviets — especially their position vis-

---

*Article 16 in the Draft which was moved forward to become Article 8 in the 1977 Constitution.

à-vis higher state organs — drew comment from local party and soviet officials and from prominent jurists as well. Thus, the chairman of the executive committee of a village soviet in the Kirgiz Republic recommended strengthening the language of the clause which empowers deputies to address inquiries to higher ranking officials or institutions (Art. 105). The official wanted to ensure that the deputy receives a reply which is "clear and timely." The deputies of the Moscow City Soviet, advised by a leading legal scientist, proposed enlarging the scope of the clause which defines the basic jurisdiction of a local soviet (Art. 146). In the same spirit, a party secretary from Tomsk Oblast suggested giving the standing committees of the local soviets a basis in constitutional law.[79]

At the same time, and with the apparent aim of increasing the accessibility of both the local soviets and individual deputies, a number of letters from ordinary citizens "below" concentrated on buttressing the provision of a deputy's accountability to constituents, contained in the basic clause that defines the role of "people's deputy" (Art. 103). For example, a citizen from Odessa proposed writing into the clause a stipulation that deputies be required to appear in person before their constituents and answer questions. Another set of proposals was aimed at ensuring the responsiveness of the executive committees of local soviets by reinforcing the requirements that they report to the local soviet as a body and, in the words of one writer, "before the population and before workers' collectives," too (Art. 149). In a related sense, still another citizen proposed extending the concept of accountability to the people's courts as well, by incorporating specific and demanding terminology in the last paragraph of the judicial election clause (Art. 152), which was largely *pro forma* as written in the Draft.[80]

Another aspect of the broad issue of participation relates to the citizen's right of criticism (Art. 49). A prominent legal scholar emphasized the importance of this right in a major article published in *Izvestiya,* and the Chairman of the Lithuanian State Committee on Television and Radio Broadcasting proposed before the Lithuanian Supreme Soviet that Article 49 be supplemented to include a requirement that officials also shall be obliged to examine and reply to citizens' proposals and requests which have been "published in the press and broadcast over television and radio."[81] The citizen's right of complaint (Art. 58) likewise received considerable attention. Two citizens wanted Article 58 to specify that "bureaucratism and red tape in the consideration of complaints" were not permitted, while an engineer from Moscow suggested making far more explicit the paragraph outlining the citizen's right to judicial remedy.[82]

Finally, there was some interest in the press in those peer justice institutions which have persisted, if on a reduced scale, since the Khrushchev period. Two writers, one a juridical scholar and the other a factory foreman, recommended that the comrades' court be mentioned specifically in the Constitution. In addition, a lead editorial in *Pravda Ukrainy* elaborately praised the people's voluntary patrols (*druzhinniki*) and suggested politely that they too should be included in the new Constitution. Neither institution had been mentioned in the Draft.[83]

"Socialist Legality" Issues

Since he assumed office in 1964, Brezhnev and his associates in the party leadership have consistently stressed the need for "law and order." Not surprisingly, this issue became a popular one in the nationwide discussion of the Draft, with the "rights and duties" and property protection clauses (Arts. 39, 59, 61) serving as special foci of attention. Several jurists and many more workers, including political activists, contributed their thoughts on both the general theme of maintaining "socialist legality" and the more specific problem of reducing economic crime. Even a few veiled, critical references to Soviet dissidents appeared. A.F. Shebanov, a distinguished legal scholar and editor of the leading Soviet law journal, *Sovetskoye gosudarstvo i pravo,* set the tone for this part of the discussion in an article in *Pravda* by characterizing "socialist law and order" as an "organic part of the Soviet way of life." One borough procurator in Moscow proposed amending Article 59 so that the citizen would be obliged "to know" as well as to observe (*soblyudat'*) the Constitution and the laws. In addition, another Moscow lawyer suggested that the citizen should be obliged to "observe" (*soblyudat'*) rather than merely "respect" (*uvazhat'*) the norms of "socialist morality" as well. This apparently was a frequent suggestion, for *Izvestiya* noted that similar recommendations had been received "from many others."[84]

Typical of the more sharply worded letters concerning economic crime was the one which suggested that Article 59 ought to include a requirement that the citizen adopt an implacable attitude toward "the psychology of private property." A number of individuals offered similar revisions of the public property protection clause (Art. 61). Thus, an army officer proposed adding a constitutional prohibition against the use of public housing for "the acquisition of unearned income." In fact, numerous letters addressed to *Izvestiya* from various parts of the Soviet Union recommended that even the personal property clause be revised to include a general prohibition against using such property for "private gain" (Art. 13).[85] Other letters concentrated on the problem of economic crime in the factories, the prime focus of the property protection clause, with suggestions that ranged from the addition of more inspirational language to reworking into a more intimidating form the phrase that threatens legal sanctions against violators of the law.[86]

The polemics between General Secretary Brezhnev and President Carter over human rights and détente during the summer of 1977[87] offered several lower party and government officials the opportunity to publicly rebut Western criticism of Soviet human rights policy, while scoring points on the "law and order" issue at the same time. In a prominent article in *Pravda,* the secretary of a party organization in the Academy of Sciences in Moscow asserted that the new Constitution exposed the "noisy campaign in defense of the rights and freedoms of citizens of the socialist states" as mere "demagogic speculation." Moreover, he recommended greatly strengthening the linkage between rights and duties in Article 59, in language which had some clearly anti-dissident overtones. A week after this was published, *Pravda* printed a small box on its discussion page which indicated that the party secretary's article had evoked considerable interest from other readers. Two of these responses were published. One, from a metal worker in Khabarovsk, referred to the dissidents as "renegades" and strongly supported the proposal to strengthen the linkage between rights and duties. In the other, a local party secretary from the Armenian SSR observed that it was "no secret that there are still citizens who opposed their personal interest to the interests of society as a whole." He, too, supported his party comrade's recommendation that "it is necessary to strengthen Article 59." Finally, a rather singular communication from Lithuania managed to touch obliquely on all aspects of the "law and order" issue. The writer, a worker and a member of the People's Voluntary Patrol, urged that the latter organization be given the authority and power to deal with "not only violations of the social order" but "anti-state acts" as well.[88]

Treatment of the "civil liberties" issue differed from the "law and order" discussion in two respects. First, civil rights was a theme of both the public discussion in the press and the "underground" discussion in *samizdat,* while "law and order" had been a topic only in the approved public forums. Second, the civil rights issue appeared to draw its support primarily from two identifiable "interest groups," one official and institutional in nature, the other decidedly unofficial and associational. In contrast, the supporters of "law and order" seemed far more diffuse.

The public discussion of civil rights had already produced a well articulated, interrelated set of proposals by the time the "underground" discussion was just beginning to surface midway in the nationwide discussion, although in the long run the scope and depth of the latter undoubtedly will eclipse the former. The jurists as a group dominated the media discussion of civil rights, while various dissidents dealt with the issue in *samizdat.* After only two months of constitutional discussion, the combined if independent efforts of jurists, ordinary citizens, and a handful of dissidents had produced commentary on 22 constitutional clauses and had raised more than two dozen specific proposals, questions, and criticisms concerning the status of civil liberties in the new Constitution. This commentary covered a wide spectrum of questions concerning both substantive and procedural due process, and several prominent jurists reopened old debates from the criminal and civil legal reforms of the late 1950's and early 1960's.

The tone of the public discussion of civil rights was set early in the summer by V.M. Savitskiy, the head of the Criminal Procedure Section of the prestigious Institute of State and Law of the USSR Academy of Sciences. He proposed emulating the East European constitutions by adding a new clause on the purpose of Soviet justice, which should be protection of the "Soviet social and state system, the rights and legal interests of citizens, as well as the rights and legal interests of state institutions and enterprises and of social organizations." More substantive concerns over due process centered first on the general socialist legality clause (Art. 4). Savitskiy pointed out that its placement at the beginning of the Constitution emphasized the significance now attached to "socialist legality." A lower-court judge in the Ukraine stressed the positive implications of the article for local soviets, in regard to their maintenance of law and order and observance of socialist legality. Nevertheless, a Moscow "shock worker" argued that the draft clause was inadequate as worded and offered a substitute version which rendered the obligation of the state and its agents to obey the Constitution and the laws in far more explicit terms.[89]

The public discussants refrained from criticizing the clauses on the substantive rights of speech, press, association, and religion (Arts. 50, 51, 52); but dissidents did not. On June 2, 1977, two days before the Draft Constitution was published, Andrey Sakharov and a group of dissidents openly appealed to the Soviet government for a "general amnesty of political prisoners" on the occasion of ratification of the forthcoming new Constitution. Implicit was criticism of the regime's practice of prosecuting dissidents for exercising their civil rights in contradiction to the officially construed caveats of the main "bill of rights" clauses (Arts. 50 and 51). The day after the Draft appeared, Sakharov announced that a "strong new wave of repression was under way" in Moscow and in the provinces.[90] On June 8, the "Christian Committee for the Defense of the Rights of Believers of the USSR" issued an appeal to Brezhnev as Chairman of the Constitutional Commission, proposing a three point resolution of the "legal crisis" for Christians that seemed implicit in the restricted "freedom of religion" clause (Art. 52).[91] First, the committee urged deleting from *party* rules the section requiring a party member to oppose "religious survivals." Next, it suggested incorporating a new statement into the party charter which would merely underscore, in principle, the incompatibility of communism and religion. Having thus proscribed religious activities and beliefs for party members, the petition continued, the party leadership should then be in a position to introduce into the text of the new Constitution a provision which allowed "the possibility in principle of religion under communism."[92]

In the published discussion, suggestions for improving operationalization of the substantive aspects of due process dominated. A pensioner and old party veteran from Azerbaidzhan, for example, believed the "right of criticism," clause (Art. 49) was too weak. Remarking that administrative suppression of criticism was dangerous for society and could lead to serious abuses, he argued that it should be not merely "prohibited" but classified as a punishable criminal offense. The well-known reform jurist, Academician M.S. Strogovich, rather eloquently elaborated the merits of the "right of complaint" article (Art. 58), but also proposed additional language for further protecting the citizen's exercise of this right. He pointed out that, under provisions of the Draft, not only did the citizen enjoy the constitutional right to make complaints, but that the state and its officials were constitutionally obligated to respond as well. Most important, he added, the judicial remedy phrase now made it possible for a citizen to turn to the courts not only in criminal and civil matters but also to remedy purely administrative abuses by government officials. Yet, to be quite certain that this important right would not be undermined, Strogovich advised adding to the clause the stipulation that "all state and social organizations shall be categorically prohibited from referring complaints for rectification to those individuals whose actions are the object of the complaint."[93]

Certain proposals were made, too, to ensure that the structure of the legal system is compatible with the full realization by citizens of their rights. For instance, G.Z. Anashkin, a former judge of the USSR Supreme Court, suggested clarifying the judicial supervision clause (Art. 153) to better ensure that the highest court would exercise effective supervision over the work of subordinate courts. Savitskiy, the criminal procedure specialist and a colleague of Strogovich, advocated substitution of a new text for the collegial decision clause (Art. 154). The revised article would include "complaints against the actions of administrative organs" within the jurisdiction of the courts. In addition, both this jurist and a "cadre inspector" from Sverdlovsk separately argued for the inclusion of more specific language in the "judicial independence" clause (Art. 155).[94] The inspector proposed increasing the responsibility of the judge and the assessors, while Savitskiy offered phrasing which would subject to prosecution anyone trying to pressure the court on a decision. Finally, former Judge Anashkin advocated decentralization of the power of pardon. This power, vested in the Presidium of the USSR Supreme Soviet by the Draft Constitution, should be extended, he argued, to the presidia of the union republic supreme soviets as well (Art. 121). But more interestingly, this jurist also urged that the clause specifying the citizen's right of complaint (Art. 58) be broadened so that individuals in custody could turn to the courts when administratively deprived of their rights by investigators and procurators in the course of the preliminary investigation.[95]

There apparently was great interest in questions of procedural due process. In fact, *Pravda* found itself the target of so many questions from readers that it decided to interview the Deputy Procurator General of the USSR, S.I. Gusev, to obtain the appropriate answers.[96] For example, a number of citizens in various parts of the Soviet Union had written asking for clarification of the right of inviolability of the home (Art. 55). The Procurator replied that, in comparison with the corresponding article in the 1936 Constitution, this right now had been clarified and strengthened, and he added that the appropriate guarantees could be found in the criminal procedure codes of the union republics. Another letterwriter's question on the privacy clause (Art. 56) received a similar response. The most

interesting question, however, came from a citizen who
noted that the personal inviolability clause (Art. 54)
essentially was identical with the same clause in the "Stalin
Constitution" and, therefore, wanted to know what
guarantees today existed that this provision would not be
violated. In reply, Gusev assured the readers that such
guarantees were now well established in the criminal codes
of the union republics.[97]

In contrast, Anashkin suggested a few days later that the
personal inviolability clause needed to be supplemented so
that not only arrest but also "detention" could only be
carried out subject to the law (Art. 54). On a somewhat
different point, Savitskiy strongly recommended combining
and greatly strengthening the two clauses which reserved the
administration of justice for the courts alone (Arts. 151 and
160). He advised inserting this synthesized statement at the
beginning of Chapter 20 on "The Courts and Arbitration,"
in place of the currently worded Article 151. Finally, the
clause providing "open" sessions for all court proceedings,
except when exempted by law (Art. 157), elicited the
criticism of a dissident who implied that this "right" had
been made a mockery of in a recent Ukrainian case and in
many other cases where the trials have actually taken place
in camera.[98]

Possibly the most important point of procedural due
process was raised by Savitskiy, the prominent Moscow
criminal proceduralist. He ended his aforementioned article
in *Izvestiya* with a strong appeal to include an explicit
presumption of innocence in the right of defense clause (Art.
158), thereby reopening, no doubt, an old debate between
"reformers" and "conservatives" within the Soviet legal
profession. In effect, he suggested that this addition would

institutionalize a meaningful right of defense in both Soviet criminal process and constitutional law. Furthermore, two letters written by jurists working as defense lawyers argued for strengthening that part of the same article that declares a defendant's right to counsel. The second letter writer, also the secretary of the party organization in a local defenders' collegium in a provincial city, proposed extending the right of defense beyond that presently provided for in Soviet criminal procedure law. He believed that the Constitution should include a citizen's right to defense counsel during the "preliminary investigation" rather than at its conclusion, thereby recalling another major issue in the earlier debates on criminal procedure reform.[99]

"Motherhood" Issues

While the civil rights issue was, for the most part, the province of lawyers and dissidents — two relatively cohesive if diametrically opposed "groups" — the "motherhood" issues seemed to stimulate the interest of *ad hoc* "lobbies." Nearly everyone, especially those specialists working in the fields, was *for* science or environmentalism. Each issue attracted an extraordinary number of letters from every part of the country and at every level of the media.

Article 26 in the Draft committed the state to ensuring the "planned development of science and the training of scientific cadres," as well as the application of the results to the economy. Scientists and technicians from every field and discipline, from research laboratories, and from teaching departments wrote to endorse this clause and propose an additional phrase or two which would tighten the "link with production," increase funding for basic research, or produce still more cadres.[100] Academicians, university presidents, and lab chiefs flooded the press with their enthusiasm for science, each one taking a few paragraphs to promote a particular specialized interest within the science community. Occasionally, a communication from a nonspecialist appeared but, even in these instances, from someone with an indirect connection with science and technology — for example, letters from a retired colonel and from a journalist polar explorer. Most of the letters, however, were written by highly educated and well-affiliated scientists.[101]

Similarly, concern for the environment proved to be an extremely popular topic in the public discussion. Specialists put forth proposals on this issue, too, but a considerable number of concerned citizens took strong environmentalist positions as well. Letters supporting the protection of nature clustered around elaborating the state's commitment (Art. 18) or strengthening the citizen's obligation (Art. 67). Many letters, such as the one from an official of the "All-Russian Society for the Protection of Nature," suggested relatively mild changes in language, although a few from average citizens advocated the inclusion of legal sanctions. While most writers promoted a general interest in environmentalism, a few seem to have had more special interests in mind, such as the forester who wanted a prohibition against poaching written into the Constitution.[102]

Constitutional Revision and Ratification

Beginning in September 1977, the public discussion of the Draft Constitution began to wind down and gradually resumed the ceremonial character of its opening weeks in June. The quieter, more formal tone was in keeping with the then approaching ratification process, and beyond, the 60th anniversary of the Bolshevik Revolution on November 7. The final communiqué of the USSR Constitutional Commission appeared in the press on September 28, signalling the official end of the nationwide discussion, both in its public and its internal, non-public forms. The brief communiqué indicated that the Commission's Secretariat, having coopted numerous specialists from the ranks of government and the universities, had managed to sift through the great volume of communications and that on the basis of its study the Commission was recommending a number of amendments to the Draft Constitution. Speaking as Chairman of the Constitutional Commission, the communiqué reported that Brezhnev had outlined the major amendments which concerned such issues as "the role of labor under socialism, a solicitous attitude toward socialist property, and the further development of socialist democracy."[103]

Just as he had dominated the process of bringing forth the Draft in the spring, Brezhnev presided over every phase of the ratification process in the fall. In sequence, he delivered the Report on the proposed revisions of the Draft before the Presidium of the USSR Supreme Soviet (September 30), a plenary session of the Central Committee (October 3), and finally before the Extraordinary Seventh Session of the Ninth USSR Supreme Soviet which convened on October 4, four months after the appearance of the Draft and on the 20th anniversary of *Sputnik* which inaugurated the space age.

In the Report published the following day throughout the USSR, Brezhnev first recited the statistics of the discussion, then outlined the major proposed amendments to the Draft, and finally, before turning to the foreign reaction to the document, discussed briefly the rejected proposals. Statistically the whole undertaking was overwhelming: 140 million people had discussed the Draft in several million meetings, all of which had produced approximately 400,000 proposals for amendments to the various articles of the Draft Constitution. Aside from purely stylistic changes, the Constitutional Commission recommended to the Supreme Soviet 150 amendments to, and textual clarifications in 110 individual articles plus the addition of one new constitutional article. In outlining the major amendments, it was clear that Brezhnev and the leadership were responding to the sociopolitical issue of participation in the nationwide discussion, as well as to the more amorphous theme of strengthening social discipline which tended to cut across the sociopolitical, "socialist legality," and, to a lesser degree, even the "motherhood" issues of the public discussion.

Finally, Brezhnev in his Report dealt swiftly with the proposals found to be "incorrect" and therefore rejected, including proposals for egalitarianism in wages and pensions, for eliminating or sharply curbing the use of the garden plot, for the abolition of the federal system and creation of a unitary state, and the "profoundly erroneous" proposals advocating the withering away of the state and the assumption by the party of its functions. Most of the offending proposals must have reached the Constitutional Commission through internal channels because few such proposals had been permitted to pass through the press' "filters" and surface in the public phase of the discussion. After a perfunctory and pro-forma three-day discussion of Brezhnev's Report and the revised Draft, the Supreme Soviet ratified the new Soviet Constitution on October 7,

1977, which henceforth became "Constitution Day," and the final text of the document was published in the major newspapers throughout the country the next day.[104]

The final text revealed the dozens of changes, stylistic and substantive, from the Preamble throughout all nine parts and 21 chapters of the document. Although few of the amendments substantially altered the Draft, the numerous changes nonetheless provided further insight into the state of Soviet "public opinion" and the points of its congruence with the party's priorities. Of the major issues which arose during the public discussion, only the reform-minded jurists' proposals on civil liberties were generally ignored by the party and the constitutional draftsmen in the revision process. At the same time, while a number of the changes were indirectly responsive to the pro-discipline impetus behind the countervailing "law and order" issue, the many illiberal proposals for strengthening the nexus between "rights and duties" were disregarded and the "linkage" clauses remained unchanged (Arts. 39 and 59).

Nearly all of the changes contributed to the further perfecting of the constitutional "housing" designed by the party to encompass the Soviet system, but generally speaking they fell into two broad categories. One set of changes tended to enlarge the interior political space or the participatory domain within the system for both individuals and institutions; while the other set of changes tended to further strengthen and reinforce the external, binding structure of the system by sealing off cracks and filling in gaps in the control and regulatory processes. The two tendencies complemented each other, the latter effecting greater system-closure, while the former pointed in the direction of "opening" up to a greater degree certain intra-system relationships and interactions.

Although some of these changes bore no observable relationship to the issue patterns discernible in the public discussion, they were apparently responsive to the internal phase of the constitutional discussion. For instance, there was little or no public commentary to foreshadow the amendments to the party hegemony clause (Art. 6), the peaceful coexistence clause (Art. 28), or the clause on state arbitration (Art. 163). In perhaps the most startling change, the party hegemony clause was supplemented by the amendment — "*All Party organizations operate within the framework of the USSR Constitution*" — raising the spectre of "limited government" in the Soviet Union (Art. 6). The full construal of the intended meaning of this interesting change will necessarily have to await the process of constitutional implementation. Less surprising and far less mysterious was the inclusion in the peaceful coexistence clause of the propaganda ploy of committing the USSR to "*general and complete disarmament*" (Art. 28). This is a familiar Soviet phrase which raises the question of why it was left out of the Draft in the first place.

While these two revisions probably came about as the result of intra-elite discussion of the Draft, the third example tended to reflect Soviet-style group politics. The state arbitrators, seeing themselves primarily as specialists in settling intra-system economic disputes, apparently preferred to be in the economic rather than the legal chapter of the Draft. Lobbying as a group through internal channels, they achieved at best a compromise. The arbitration clause remained where it was originally in the Draft, but was amended to stipulate that the basic operation of the arbitration system would be defined by an all-union statute

(Art. 163). This, in turn, opened up new vistas for future lobbying efforts by the arbitrators to amend their governing statute in the direction of changing their de facto status in the constitutional order.

However, more often than expected, changes in the final text of the Constitution of 1977 were traceable to the general themes which shaped the public portion of the discussion of the Draft. Basically, the constitutional draftsmen revised and amended the Draft in response to the very widely expressed desire for broader and more dependable opportunities for both individual and institutional participation in the process of implementing party policy and state legislation, as well as to the intensely felt demands for more and stricter discipline throughout the society. This two-fold response to public opinion can be seen initially in the changes and emendations to the Preamble. The advocates of increased participation undoubtedly appreciated the addition of the open-ended concept of "communist social self government," a holdover from Khrushchev's days which carries with it the implication of comrades' courts, people's voluntary patrols, people's control commissions, and other vehicles of mass participation. Similarly, the social disciplinarians were no doubt pleased with the strengthened linkage concept by which citizens' "rights and liberties" were interconnected not merely with the performance of their "civic responsibility" as in the Draft Preamble, but with "*their duties and responsibility to society*" in the final text. To drive the point home, the linkage concept was also inserted in the revised conclusion of the Preamble which "*proclaim*[s]" the linkage of rights and duties among other ideas as the core of the new Constitution.[105]

The Participation Amendments

Most of the participation-oriented amendments to the Draft Constitution appear to have been designed to have an effect on both mass and elite participatory structures and processes, as well as on the accountability procedures by which constituent groups at different levels in the system obtain knowledge of their elected representatives' actions. Essentially, these changes were addressed more to the quantitative aspects of participation (how much can occur) rather than the qualitative side of the issue (how effective it may be). The increased participatory emphasis was dramatically keynoted in the opening articles of the final document as the expanded worker's participation clause was moved up from the economic chapter (Art. 16 of the Draft) to the political chapter (Art. 8 of the Constitution). The theoretical increase of mass participation in lower-level economic decision-making was paralleled by the one new article added to the Draft which constitutionally legitimated the citizen's right of indirect participation in local policymaking by elevating to full constitutional status the concept of the "*voters' mandates*" (Art. 102). In addition, the clause on the citizen's general right of participation in national policymaking was recast and strengthened, particularly with reference to the greater emphasis on the mass public's right to participate "*in the discussion and adoption of laws and decision of nationwide and local importance*" (Art. 48). This tendency was complemented by the increased attention to the concept of the nationwide "*referendum*" (Arts. 108, 115, and 137), and the empowering of the USSR Supreme Soviet to submit for nationwide discussion not just "draft laws," but also "*other very important questions of state life*" (Art. 114).

Governmental bodies, as well as voters and workers, also received enhanced constitutional attention to their participatory status. The powers of local soviets, autonomous republics, and union republics were all enlarged to include ensuring "*comprehensive economic and social development*" on their territories (Arts. 147, 83, and 77). In addition, each governmental strata, respectively, gained greater supervisory authority over enterprises and other institutions of higher subordination on its territory, all of which represented a commitment by the Soviet leadership to a slightly greater degree of decentralization by means of creating considerably more decision-making space for subordinate governmental levels within the system (Arts. 147, 83, 77, and 142).

Making the various representational strata of the government more accessible and accountable to their respective constituencies, at least in terms of periodic information about their activities, was the other aspect of the intensified stress on the participatory motif. As a result, a people's deputy is now obliged to report on his work not just to his constituents, but "*also to the collectives and public organizations that nominated him as a candidate for Deputy*" (Art. 107). In turn, the executive committees of the local soviets must not only report to their soviets at least once a year, but "*to meetings of labor collectives and of citizens at their places of residence*" as well (Art. 149). Another amendment enjoins the "*Soviets of People's Deputies and the agencies created by them [to] systematically inform the population about their work and the decisions they adopt*" (Art. 94). Even judges and people's assessors or co-judges have now been explicitly required to "*report*" on their work from time to time to "the voters or the agencies that elected them" (Art. 152).

Ascending the bureaucratic hierarchy, the higher administrative bodies as well were made, theoretically at least, more accountable to the legislative branch of government. This was accomplished by amending the clause on standing committees of the USSR Supreme Soviet to read:

The committees' recommendations are subject to mandatory consideration by state and public agencies, institutions and organizations. Reports are to be made to the committees, within established time periods, on the results of such consideration or on the measures taken (Art. 125).

Last, but hardly least, the right of criticism clause (Art. 49) was significantly amended in a way that bridged both the themes of participation and discipline in the discussion of the Draft Constitution. To better facilitate and protect citizen participation and to help ensure official adherence to the requirements of administrative legality, the existing prohibition against officials persecuting their critics was noticeably strengthened to read: "*Persons who persecute others for criticism will be called to account*" (Art. 49). If faithfully executed, this amendment alone could well prove to be the most important revision of the Draft in terms of making the Soviet system somewhat more responsive to the concerns of the individual citizen. Most likely, however, the "criticism" clause probably contains an implied "catch" to the effect that only "constructive" criticism will be afforded constitutional protection from retaliatory persecution. Under the best of circumstances, reasonable men will differ over what constitutes "constructive" criticism in a given situation; therefore, a safe conjecture would be that generally neither dissidents nor even persistent "whistleblowers" should expect too much from the amended safeguards in this clause.

New Constitutional Duties

Considerably less ambiguous are the additional constitutional directives addressed to the Soviet citizen in his various roles. On top of the maze of overlapping obligations imposed on the citizen in the Draft Constitution, amendments provided for nine new or reinforced duties. These can be grouped together as the party's and the draftsmen's response to the strongly articulated and widespread demands for more discipline of all kinds cutting across the three sets of issues that had dominated the nationwide public discussion. Although largely rhetorical and frequently unenforceable, these new constitutional burdens qualify the Soviet citizen as one of the most constitutionally-bound individuals of modern times.

In the final, official text of the 1977 Constitution, children are enjoined to "*help*" their parents (Art. 66), residents to "*take good care*" of their housing (Art. 44), and all able-bodied persons are expected to engage in "*socially useful labor*" (Art. 60). Individuals may now only use their personal property (Art. 13) or engage in "individual labor activity" in the "*interests of society*" (Art. 17), and those people assigned garden plots are directed "*to make rational use*" of them (Art. 13). All adults are cautioned against using socialist property for "*selfish purposes*" (Art. 10), while collective farmers "*are obliged to use land effectively*" (Art. 12), and workers are instructed "*to take good care of the people's property*" (Art. 61). In addition, everyone's civic duty to help save historical monuments has been semantically reinforced and enshrined in a separate article in the final text of the new Constitution (Art. 68). Finally, all citizens are put on notice that their exercise of the civil liberties of speech, press, and assembly must now not only contribute to the "strengthening" but also to the "*developing*" of the socialist system as well (Art. 50).

Aside from the new constitutional strictures on land use, the "motherhood" issues of science (Art. 26) and environmentalism (Arts. 18 and 67) received only nominal attention in the constitutional revision process, despite the avalanche of proposals on these issues. "*Water resources*" were brought under the umbrella of environmental protection (Art. 18), the citizen's "protective" duties became the sole focus of a single constitutional article (Art. 67), and the state's vast legislative and executive powers were marginally amended to include environmental and science legislation among its myriad other responsibilities (Art. 73, Sec. 5; and Art. 131, Sec. 7).

Succinctly summarizing the process of revising the Draft into the new Soviet Constitution of 1977, the party has skillfully exploited the existing illiberal currents of public opinion to justify the near completion of its theoretical closure of the Soviet system, while constitutionally acknowledging the participatory impulse "from below" through incremental adjustments and marginal changes, the realization of which awaits implementation.

The Constitution as "Magic Wall"

The number of individuals who participated in the discussion and the nature of many of their suggestions indicated that many Soviet citizens are attentive to — and may even take seriously — the potentially prescriptive aspects of their new Constitution. While their perceptions may prove to be unjustified, they do serve, implicitly, as "public support" for the more normative Constitution envisioned by the "constitutionalist" scholars. More important, the extent to which the 1977 Constitution does function as a prescriptive document will provide a benchmark for measuring the scope and limits of change in the Soviet polity.

In a more fundamental sense, however, the new Constitution still represents the sedimentation of six decades of Soviet rule. This Constitution is a distillation of that cumulative experience, although it also serves to codify the shifting emphasis from rule by force to rule by law that has emerged since Josef Stalin's death a quarter of a century ago. The result is a Soviet-style *Rechtsstaat,* a legal framework through which the party can govern its vast domain without irrevocably limiting its ultimate power of action. In essence, the Brezhnev regime has created in constitutional form a "magic wall" which conceals the "close cohabitation between wide stretches of certainty for mass man's daily living conditions and unheard of areas of oppression [and] lawlessness."[106]

Footnotes

[1] *Pravda* (Moscow), May 25, 1977, p. 1; and *ibid.,* June 17, 1977, p. 1. For the Constitutional Commission's brief communiqué, see *ibid.,* May 24, 1977, p. 1. The Draft was subsequently published on June 4 throughout the national and regional press. See the translation in *Current Digest of the Soviet Press* (hereafter *CDSP*), June 29, 1977, pp. 1-11, 22.

Podgornyy did not appear in person before the Supreme Soviet; his "resignation" was made in his behalf. In addition, the May plenum also relieved Konstantin Katushev from his post as Central Committee Secretary supervising relations with ruling Communist parties. He was replaced by K.V. Rusakov, in a change apparently unrelated to the decision to publish the new Constitution.

[2] The growing constitutional discussion in short order subsumed both the campaign preceding the local soviet elections, scheduled for June 19, and the socialist competitions in honor of the then forthcoming 60th anniversary celebration. See *Pravda,* June 20, 1977, for coverage of the elections. For a typical "socialist emulation" pledge by a factory in response to the constitutional discussion, see *Ekonomicheskaya gazeta* (Moscow), No. 28, 1977, p. 4. On the constitutional revision and ratification process, see *Pravda* and *Izvestiya* (Moscow), September 28-October 8, 1977. The final text of the new Constitution appeared in the issues for October 8, 1977.

For a translation of the final, official text of the new Soviet Constitution of 1977, see *CDSP,* November 9, 1977, pp. 1-13, reprinted in this volume at p. 73. The translator's italics and brackets have been retained to indicate where, respectively, additions to and deletions from the earlier Draft text were made in the final document.

[3] On the drafting, discussion, and ratification of the 1936 Constitution see S.I. Rusinova and V.A. Ryanzhin, eds., *Sovetskoye konstitutsionnoye pravo* (Soviet Constitutional Law) (Leningrad: Izdatel'stvo Leningradskogo Universiteta, 1975), pp. 75-79. Since December 5, 1965, "Constitution Day" has also been the occasion for an annual silent-protest demonstration by human rights dissidents in Moscow's Pushkin Square. See *A Chronicle of Human Rights in the USSR,* No. 23-24, October-December 1976, p. 10.

[4] See Robert C. Tucker, "Stalinism as Revolution from Above," and Moshe Lewin, "The Social Background of Stalinism," both in Robert C. Tucker, ed., *Stalinism: Essays in Historical Interpretation* (New York: Norton, 1977), pp. 77-108 and 111-36, respectively.

[5] See the 1936 Constitution, Arts. 1, 2, 7, 9, and 10. For an English translation see Harold J. Berman and John B. Quigley, Jr., eds., *Basic Laws on*

the Structure of the Soviet State (Cambridge: Harvard University Press, 1969), pp. 3-28.

[6]For a summary of the constitutional revision process from World War II through 1970, see John N. Hazard, "Soviet Law and Justice," in John W. Strong, ed., *The Soviet Union Under Brezhnev and Kosygin* (New York: Van Nostrand, 1971), esp. pp. 109-14. For an authoritative account by a leading Soviet legal scholar of the constitutional proposals under discussion prior to the creation of Khrushchev's constitutional commission, see P.S. Romashkin, "New Stage in the Development of the Soviet State," *Sovetskoye gosudarstvo i pravo* (Moscow), October 1960, pp. 31-40. A *CDSP* translation of this important article is reprinted in Jan F. Triska, ed., *Constitutions of the Communist Party-States* (Stanford: Hoover Institution, 1968), pp. 77-87. Several of the major ideas outlined by Romashkin in 1960 are included in the Constitution ratified 17 years later. For a Western analysis of the various proposals for constitutional revision before the creation of Khrushchev's commission in 1962, see George Ginsburgs, "A Khrushchev Constitution: Projects and Prospects," *Osteuropa Recht* (Cologne), August 1962, pp. 191-214.

[7]See Jerome S. Gilison, "Khrushchev, Brezhnev, and Constitutional Reform," *Problems of Communism,* September-October 1972, esp. pp. 75-78.

[8]See Hazard, "Soviet Law and Justice," in Strong, *op. cit.,* p. 111.

[9]L.I. Brezhnev, "Report of the CPSU Central Committee and the Immediate Tasks of the Party in Home and Foreign Policy," *XXVth Congress of the CPSU* (Moscow: Novosti, 1976), pp. 101-02. For the "echo" in the legal press, see, e.g., the unsigned lead article, "The 25th Congress of the CPSU: Further Development of the Soviet State, Democracy, and Law," *Sovetskoye gosudarstvo i pravo,* No. 5, May 1976, esp. pp. 7-8.

[10]Shortly after publication of the Draft Constitution, Politburo member G.V. Romanov, First Secretary of the Leningrad Obkom and a member of the Constitutional Commission, reported that the Draft had been discussed "repeatedly" in the Politburo, Central Committee Secretariat, Constitutional Commission, and various state institutions. To some extent, he attributed the length of the drafting process to the thoroughness with which the constitutional principles were discussed in these different forums. He noted that many well-known Soviet scholars were consulted during the drafting process, including historians, jurists, philosophers, and sociologists, as well as representatives of the mass social organizations. At the same time, he also made specific reference to Brezhnev's "initiative [in the decision] to approve (*prinyat'*) this historic document in the year of the 60th anniversary of the Great October. . . ." See *Leningradskaya pravda* (Leningrad), June 9, 1977, p. 2.

[11]For translations of the 1918 and 1924 Constitutions, see Triska, *op. cit.,* pp. 2-36.

[12]*Pravda,* June 5, 1977, pp. 1-2. Brezhnev's Report was published verbatim in the national and regional press on June 5, one day after publication of the Draft Constitution. For a translation, see *CDSP,* July 6, 1977, pp. 6-10.

[13]For environmental legislation, see, e.g., *Fundamentals of Legislation of the USSR and the Union Republics* (Moscow: Progress Publishers, 1974), pp. 15-16 and 39-40. Also, see Zigurds L. Zile, "Soviet Struggle for Environmental Quality: The Limits of Environmental Law Under Central Planning," in Donald D. Barry, et al., eds., *Contemporary Soviet Law: Essays in Honor of John N. Hazard* (The Hague: Martinus Nijhoff, 1974), pp. 124-57.

For recent Soviet perspectives on international law, see G.I. Tunkin, *Theory of International Law,* tr. by William E. Butler (Cambridge: Harvard University Press, 1974), especially Chapters 2 and 3. Tunkin is a former diplomat and the leading Soviet scholar on international law.

On labor legislation, see the Fundamental Principles of Labor Legislation, in *Fundamentals of Legislation of the USSR,* p. 91. On the labor law reforms generally, see A.K.R. Kiralfy, "Soviet Labor Law Reform Since Stalin," in Barry, et al., eds., *Contemporary Soviet Law,* pp. 158-74.

[14]Nikita S. Khrushchev, "The Crimes of the Stalin Era — Special Report to the 20th Congress of the Communist Party of the Soviet Union," *The New Leader,* Supplement, July 16, 1956, p. s63.

[15]Although, as we shall see, this is not the case with respect to the Soviet Union's political, religious, ethnic, and cultural dissidents. See M.S. Strogovich, "On the Rights of the Individual in Soviet Criminal Procedure," *Sovetskoye gosudarstvo i pravo,* No. 10, October 1976, pp. 73-81, and translated in *Soviet Review,* Vol. 18, No. 2, Summer 1977, pp. 3-17. On civil process, see Donald D. Barry, "The Specialist in Soviet Policy-Making: The Adoption of a Law," *Soviet Studies,* October 1964, pp. 152-65; and Whitmore Gray, "Soviet Tort Law: The New Principles Annotated," *University of Illinois Law Forum,* Spring 1964, pp. 180-211.

[16]On the duality of legality and extra-legality, see Robert Sharlet, "Stalinism and Soviet Legal Culture," in Tucker, ed., *Stalinism,* pp. 155-79.

[17]The "state law" school continues to be heavily represented in the Soviet academic legal establishment, although the late Professor A.I. Lepeshkin was probably its most influential spokesman. His *Kurs Sovetskogo gosudarstvennogo prava* (A Treatise on Soviet State Law), Vol. 1 (Moscow: Yuridicheskaya literatura, 1961), was a basic reference in the debate that emerged in the early 1960's. The early leader of the "constitutionalists" was the late V.F. Kotok who broke new ground in contemporary

Soviet jurisprudence with his introductory essay to the book he edited with N.P. Farberov, *Konstitutsionnoye pravo sotsialisticheskikh stran* (Constitutional Law of the Socialist States) (Moscow: Akademiya Nauk SSSR, 1963). Kotok's article was sharply criticized in the legal press and at a special meeting of the faculty and graduate students of the Department of State Law and Soviet Construction at Moscow University Law School during the academic year 1963-64. The next major position statement of the "constitutional law" school was I.E. Farber and V.A. Rzhevskiy's *Voprosy teorii Sovetskogo konstitutsionnogo prava* (Theoretical Questions of Soviet Constitutional Law), No. 1 (Saratov: Saratovskiy yuridicheskiy institut, 1967). For a subsequent statement of the orthodox position, see B.V. Shchetinin, *Problemy teorii Sovetskogo gosudarstvennogo prava* (Theoretical Problems of Soviet State Law), Part I (Moscow: Yuridicheskaya literatura, 1969), and Part II, published in 1974. Compare this to the latest and most authoritative statement of the "constitutionalists," Rusinova and Ryanzhin, *Sovetskoye konstitutsionnoye pravo, op. cit.* For an account of the unfavorable reception which this last study received at a special meeting of legal scholars, held under the auspices of the Department of State Law and Soviet Construction at Moscow University Law School in February 1976, see N.A. Mikhaleva, "The Discussion of the Book *Soviet Constitutional Law,*" *Vestnik Moskovskogo Universiteta: Pravo* (Moscow), July-August 1976, pp. 86-90. The rapporteur is a member of the "state law" school. For a Western article which points out the Rusinova and Ryanzhin volume's implications for the process of Soviet constitutional reform, see Christopher Osakwe's review essay in *Tulane Law Review,* Vol. 51, 1977, pp. 411-22.

[18]In spite of the already noted hostile reaction to the constitutionalists' latest statement, the author was told by a reliable source that even before publication of the new Draft Constitution, several leading representatives of the "old guard" had conceded privately, albeit reluctantly, that the concept of "constitutional law" had won the day in Soviet jurisprudence. If this in fact is the case, the "victory" should soon be consolidated by changes in law school curricula, and, eventually, the disciplinary/departmental name "state law" should be at least supplemented with the phrase "constitutional law."

[19]For a conceptual analysis of metapolicy and *ad hoc* action as legal policy, see Robert Sharlet, "Soviet Legal Policymaking: A Preliminary Classification," in a special issue edited by Harry M. Johnson, "Social System and Legal Process," *Sociological Inquiry,* Vol. 47, Nos. 3-4, 1977, esp. pp. 212-14 and 218-19.

[20]See, e.g., V.M. Chkhikvadze et al., eds., *Politicheskaya organizatsiya Sovetskogo obshchestva* (The Political Organization of Soviet Society) (Moscow: Nauka, 1967); and M.N. Marchenko, *Demokraticheskiye*

osnovy politicheskoy organizatsii Sovetskogo obshchestva (The Democratic Principles of the Political Organization of Soviet Society) (Moscow: Izdatel'stvo Moskovskogo Universiteta, 1977).

[21]In a seminal essay written nearly a decade ago, Richard Lowenthal argued that advancing socioeconomic modernization seems to make this shift inevitable. See his "Development versus Utopia in Communist Policy," in Chalmers Johnson, ed., *Change in Communist Systems* (Stanford: Stanford University Press, 1970), pp. 33-116. For his recent analysis of the dilemmas which modernization creates for one-party systems, see "The Ruling Party in a Mature Society," in Mark Field, ed., *Social Consequences of Modernization in Communist Societies* (Baltimore: The Johns Hopkins University Press, 1976), pp. 81-118.

[22]Article 9 reads: "Further development of socialist democracy constitutes the basic direction in the evolution of the political system of Soviet society: [that is] the ever wider participation of working people in the management of the affairs of society and government; the improvement of the state apparatus; a heightening of the activeness of public organizations; the strengthening of the people's control; the reinforcement of the legal foundations of state and public life; the expansion of publicity; [and] the continual regard for public opinion." (Author's translation.)

[23]See Roger E. Kanet, "The Rise and Fall of the 'All-People's State': Recent Changes in the Soviet Theory of the State," *Soviet Studies,* July 1968, pp. 81-93. Years of doctrinal paring have stripped the Khrushchevian concept of its emphasis on the "withering away" of the state through the transfer of selected state functions to mass organizations of "social self-government." The contemporary concept merely envisions limited democratization of the Soviet political system through a somewhat greater participation of mass social organizations as collective entities. See, e.g., B.N. Topornin, "The All-People's State and Socialist Democracy," *Pravovedeniye* (Leningrad), March-April 1975, pp. 7-17.

[24]See Stalin Constitution, Art. 130.

[25]See Peter H. Juviler, *Revolutionary Law and Order: Politics and Social Change in the USSR* (New York: Free Press, 1976), pp. 85-116.

[26]See Stalin Constitution, Arts. 126 and 141.

[27]Cf. *ibid.,* Arts. 4-12.

[28]I am indebted to Professor John Hazard of Columbia Law School for alerting me to this change of wording, as well as for several other helpful suggestions in connection with this article. For a complementary analysis of the new Soviet Constitution, see his "A Constitution for 'Developed Socialism,'" in George Ginsburgs, Peter B. Maggs, and Donald D. Barry, eds., *Social Engineering Through Law in the Soviet Union* (Leiden: A.W. Sijthoff, forthcoming).

[29]Cf. Stalin Constitution, Art. 11.

[30]See *Sotsialisticheskoye sorevnovaniye v SSSR 1918-1964* (Socialist Competition in the USSR, 1918-1964) (Moscow: Profizdat, 1965), pp. 127-40 and Part Three. Also see Erik P. Hoffmann, "The 'Scientific Management' of Soviet Society," *Problems of Communism,* May-June 1977, pp. 59-67; and Robert F. Miller, "The Scientific-Technical Revolution and the Soviet Administrative Debate," in Paul Cocks, Robert V. Daniels, and Nancy Whittier Heer, eds., *The Dynamics of Soviet Politics* (Cambridge: Harvard University Press, 1976), pp. 137-55.

[31]Cf. Stalin Constitution, Art. 12. See also R. Beermann, "The Parasite Law in the Soviet Union," *British Journal of Criminology,* Vol. 3, 1962, pp. 71-80.

[32]See "The 1961 Programme of the Communist Party of the Soviet Union," in Jan F. Triska, ed., *Soviet Communism: Programs and Rules* (San Francisco: Chandler, 1962), esp. Part Two, pp. 68-122.

[33]*Ibid.,* pp. 35-39 and 63-67.

[34]Article 29 includes "Basket Three," or the human rights principles, of the Helsinki document. Cf. "Conference on Security and Cooperation in Europe: Final Act," *The Department of State Bulletin* (Washington, D.C.: Government Printing Office, September 1, 1975), pp. 323-50. From the Soviet perspective, these principles must be looked at within the context of Part II of the Constitution, on "The State and the Individual." The "Brezhnev doctrine" is covered in Article 30 in the guise of "comradely mutual assistance."

[35]Cf. Stalin Constitution, Art. 14.

[36]Cf. *ibid.,* Arts. 118-22.

[37]In a June 1977 session at the Kennan Institute (Washington, D.C.) devoted to a discussion of the Draft Constitution, Professor Moshe Lewin characterized the cluster of economic and other rights as descriptive of a "super welfare state," based on an obligation to work. For the details of Soviet health care legislation, see the Fundamental Principles of Health Legislation of 1969 in *Fundamentals of Legislation of the USSR,* pp. 62-88. The new article on old age maintenance has been elaborated in practice by a developing body of pension law. See, for example, M.L. Zakharov, ed., *Sovetskoye pensionnoye pravo* (Soviet Pension Law) (Moscow: Yuridich-eskaya literatura, 1974).

[38]See Stalin Constitution, Art. 131. On the contemporary problem of economic crime, see, e.g., Gregory Grossman, "The 'Second Economy' of the USSR," *Problems of Communism,* September-October, 1977, pp. 25-40; and Valery Chalidze, *Criminal Russia: Essays on Crime in the Soviet Union* (New York: Random House, 1977), Chs. 8-10.

[39]Cf. *ibid.,* Arts. 125-26.

[40]Cf. *ibid.,* Art. 130.

[41]I believe it is misleading to describe the "linkage" of rights and duties as the regime's "answer" to the dissidents. For an argument in this direction, see "New USSR Draft Constitution," *International Commission of Jurists Review* (Geneva), June 1977, p. 30. Rather, the nexus of rights and duties is a general principle in contemporary Soviet legislation. See, e.g., the Land Fundamentals, Art. 11, and the Civil Fundamentals, Art. 5, in *Fundamentals of Legislation of the USSR,* pp. 15-16 and 153-54, respectively.

[42]*Ibid.,* pp. 271-99. See also, John Gorgone, "Soviet Jurists in the Legislative Arena: The Reform of Criminal Procedure, 1956-1958," *Soviet Union,* Vol. 3, Part 1, 1976, pp. 1-35; and Harold J. Berman's Introduction to Berman and James W. Spindler, eds., *Soviet Criminal Law and Procedure: The RSFSR Codes,* 2nd ed. (Cambridge: Harvard University Press, 1972), esp. pp. 47-70 and 84-89.

[43]See Christopher Osakwe, "Due Process of Law Under Contemporary Soviet Criminal Procedure," *Tulane Law Review,* Vol. 50, 1976, pp. 266-317. Nine such "cases" were translated by Harold Berman in *Soviet Statutes and Decisions,* Summer 1965, pp. 5-41. Numerous others are translated in John N. Hazard, William E. Butler, and Peter B. Maggs, eds., *The Soviet Legal System: Fundamental Principles and Historical Commentary,* 3rd ed. (Dobbs Ferry, NY: Oceana, 1977), Ch. 7.

[44]Cf. Stalin Constitution, Art. 127. See also the Criminal Procedural Fundamentals, Art. 6, in *Fundamentals of Legislation of the USSR,* p. 274; the RSFSR Criminal Procedure Code, Art. 11, in Berman, *Soviet Criminal Law and Procedure,* p. 209; Berman's analysis of the personal inviolability articles in *ibid.,* pp. 48-50; and the Bortkevich case in Hazard et al.,*The Soviet Legal System,* pp. 112-113.

[45]See Stalin Constitution, Art. 102. The "special courts" were transportation courts with jurisdiction over criminal offenses that took place on the railway and water transport system. They were abolished in the post-Stalin era and are not mentioned in the Fundamental Principles of Legislation on the Court System. See *Fundamentals of Legislation of the USSR,* Art. 1, p. 137. On contemporary "special courts" which have special legal personnel and jurisdiction over individuals engaged in classified work, see Yury Luryi, "The Admittance of the Defence Counsel to Common Criminal (Non-Political) Cases in Soviet Criminal Procedure as the Most Essential Part of the Right of the Defendant for Defence," paper read at the annual meeting of the American Association for the Advancement of Slavic Studies (AAASS), St. Louis, Missouri, October 7, 1976.

[46]On the class approach to justice and its abandonment, see John N. Hazard, "Reforming Soviet Criminal Law," *Journal of Criminal Law and Criminology,* July-August 1938, pp. 157-69.

[47]Cf. Stalin Constitution, Art. 111. For analysis of the changing status of

the Soviet defense counsel, see Jean C. Love, "The Role of Defense Counsel in Soviet Criminal Proceedings," *Wisconsin Law Review*, No. 3, 1968, pp. 806-900; and Lawrence M. Friedman and Zigurds L. Zile, "Soviet Legal Profession: Recent Developments in Law and Practice," *ibid.*, No. 1, 1964, pp. 32-77. The mass organizations may also assign a "social accuser" to assist a procurator in a criminal case. For a brief analysis of both social accusers and defenders, see Berman, *Soviet Criminal Law and Procedure*, pp. 69-70.

[48]See John N. Hazard, *Settling Disputes in Soviet Society: The Formative Years of Legal Institutions* (New York: Columbia University Press, 1960), pp. 34-35, 47-49, 159-62.

[49]The "open court" clause specifies: "The examination of cases in all courts is open. The hearing of cases in closed court is permitted only in instances provided for by law, and then with the observance of all the rules of judicial procedure." (Author's translation.)

[50]Harold J. Berman, *Justice in the USSR,* rev. ed. (Cambridge: Harvard University Press, 1963), p. 70.

[51]*Pravda*, June 5, 1977, p. 1.

[52]Except for "political" cases, in which *partiynost'* (party-mindedness) routinely supersedes *zakonnost'* (legality), the following statement by a Soviet university lecturerer seems to characterize the administration of justice in the post-Stalin period: "The party organs oversee the selection, placement, and ideological education of juridical cadres. But, at the same time, any kind of interference in the administration of justice in specific cases is absolutely ruled out." *Pravda,* August 19, 1977, p. 3. See also the author's review of Samuel Kucherov's *The Organs of Soviet Administration of Justice* in *Columbia Law Review,* Vol. 71, No. 7, November 1971, esp. pp. 1346-48.

[53]See Stalin Constitution, Art. 113. The corresponding passage in the 1977 Constitution is more specific and emphatic and appears at the beginning of a separate chapter on the Procuracy (Ch. 21). For a history of the Procuracy's functions under Stalin, see Glen G. Morgan, *Soviet Administrative Legality: The Role of the Attorney General's Office* (Stanford: Stanford University Press, 1962), pp. 76-126.

[54]See the 13 cases analyzed in Christopher Osakwe, "Due Process of Law and Civil Rights Cases in the Soviet Union," in Donald D. Barry, George Ginsburgs, and Peter B. Maggs, eds., *Law Reform Under Khrushchev and Brezhnev* (Leiden: A.W. Sijthoff, 1978). Even in ordinary (nonpolitical) cases, however, a "major retreat of the due process function in favor of the crime control function" has taken place at least temporarily during the various anti-crime campaigns under Khrushchev and Brezhnev. See Stanislaw Pomorski, "Criminal Law Protection of Socialist Property in the USSR," in *ibid.*

[55]See Max Hayward, ed., *On Trial: The Soviet State versus 'Abram Tertz' and 'Nikolai Arzhak,'* rev. and enlarged ed. (New York: Harper and Row, 1967). See also Robert Sharlet, "Dissent and Repression in the Soviet Union," *Current History,* October 1977, pp. 112-17 and 130.

[56]Harold J. Berman, "The Educational Role of Soviet Criminal Law and Civil Procedure," in Barry et al., *Contemporary Soviet Law,* pp. 14-16. The literature on violations of dissidents' rights is voluminous. See, e.g., Christopher Osakwe, "Due Process of Law and Civil Rights Cases in the Soviet Union," *loc. cit.,* for a detailed and systematic analysis of the due process violations reported in political cases; and *A Chronicle of Human Rights in the USSR,* for continuing unofficial documentation of Soviet political "justice."

[57]For recent examples of the "legalist" strategy see Valery Chalidze, *To Defend These Rights: Human Rights and the Soviet Union* (New York: Random House, 1974); and the "legalist" analyses of Soviet constitutional law, prior to publication of the Draft Constitution, by Henn-Juri Uibopuu and Alexander Volpin in Leon Lipson and Valery Chalidze, eds., *Papers on Soviet Law* (New York: Institute on Socialist Law, 1977), pp. 14-51 and 52-107, respectively. For a "legalist" analysis of the Draft Constitution, see Sofia Kallistratova, "Comments on the Draft Constitution," *A Chronicle of Human Rights in the USSR,* No. 27, July-September 1977, pp. 56-64. This critique appeared in the West via *samizdat* just after the 1977 Constitution was ratified.

[58]For the pertinent post-Stalin legislation on tort liability, see the Civil Fundamentals, Ch. 12, in *Fundamentals of Legislation in the USSR,* pp. 188-90; enactment of the Civil Fundamentals in the RSFSR Civil Code of 1964, Ch. 40, in Whitmore Gray and Raymond Stults, eds., *Civil Code of the Russian Soviet Federal Socialist Republic* (Ann Arbor: University of Michigan Law School, 1965), pp. 117-24; and the analysis of the Principles, code law, and selected cases in Donald D. Barry, "The Soviet Union," in Donald D. Barry, ed., *Governmental Tort Liability in the Soviet Union, Bulgaria . . . and Yugoslavia* (Leiden: A.W. Sijthoff, 1970), pp. 54-70.

[59]*Pravda,* June 5, 1977, p. 2. The following account of the constitutional discussion was based on a survey of articles and letters about the Draft Constitution published from June 4 through mid-September 1977, in the following newspapers: *Pravda, Izvestiya, Vechernyaya Moskva* (Moscow), *Literaturnaya gazeta* (Moscow), and *Ekonomicheskaya gazeta.* In addition, six other national and republican newspapers were surveyed intermittently during the same period: *Komsomol'skaya pravda* (Moscow), *Krasnaya zvezda* (Moscow), *Sovetskaya Litva* (Vilnius), *Pravda Ukrainy* (Kiev), *Bakinskiy rabochiy* (Baku), and *Leningradskaya pravda.*

[60]See, e.g., G.V. Romanov's report to the *aktiv* of the Leningrad party organization, *Leningradskaya pravda,* June 9, 1977, p. 2; *Pravda's* lead

editorial, June 9, 1977, p. l; and P.P. Grishkyavichus' report to the Lithuanian Supreme Soviet, in *Sovetskaya Litva,* July 3, 1977, p. 1. Grishkyavichus is First Secretary of the Central Committee of the Lithuanian Communist Party and, like Romanov, was elected a member of the Constitutional Commission in April 1977.

[61]*Pravda,* June 7, 1977, p. 1.

[62]*Ibid.,* June 5, 1977, p. 2.

[63]See, e.g., *Pravda's* lead editorial, June 6, 1977, p. 1; Romanov's remarks of June 9, 1977, *loc. cit.;* and Sh. R. Rashidov's report to the *aktiv* of the Uzbek republic party organization, *Pravda,* June 10, 1977, p. 3. Rashidov is First Secretary of the Central Committee of the Uzbek Communist Party and a member of the CPSU Politburo.

[64]June 9, 1977, p. 1. This theme was reiterated in *Pravda's* lead editorial of June 29, 1977, p. 1.

[65]The following description is based in part on several conversations the author had with well-informed persons.

[66]See Christian Duevel, "A Secretive Reorganization of the Constitutional Commission," *Radio Liberty Research,* RL 141/77, June 7, 1977, especially pp. 2, 4, and 6-8; and *Vedomosti Verkhovnogo Soveta SSSR* (Moscow), No. 18 (1884), May 4, 1977, Item 274.

[67]See Robert Sharlet, "Concept Formation in Political Science and Communist Studies: Conceptualizing Political Participation," in Frederic J. Fleron, Jr., ed., *Communist Studies and the Social Sciences* (Chicago: Rand McNally, 1969), pp. 244-53.

[68]See, e.g., *Pravda,* June 11, 1977, p. 3; *Ibid.,* June 13, p. 3; and V.V. Grishin's article in *ibid.,* June 14, pp. 2-3. Grishin is First Secretary of the Moscow City Party Committee and a member of the Politburo. See also the article by the Chairman of the Presidium of the Ukrainian Supreme Soviet in *Izvestiya,* June 14, 1977, p. 2.

[69]*Izvestiya,* July 8, 1977, p. 2; and *Pravda Ukrainy,* July 3, 1977, p. 2. Subsequently, the Constitutional Commission reported that through July 20, 1977, more than 650,000 meetings of working collectives had been held, involving 57,000,000 people. See *Izvestiya,* July 30, 1977, p. 1.

[70]See *Izvestiya,* July 10, 1977, p. 2; and *ibid.,* July 15, 1977, p. 2.

[71]*Pravda,* July 9, 1977, p. 3.

[72]In the context of electoral politics, these have been called "valence-issues." See Donald E. Stokes, "Spatial Models of Party Competition," in Angus Campbell et al., *Elections and the Political Order* (New York: Wiley, 1966), pp. 161-79.

[73]*ravda,* July 13, 1977, p. 1; and *Komsomol'skaya pravda,* July 14, 1977, p. 1.

[74] *Pravda,* July 18, 1977, p. 3; *Izvestiya,* July 19, 1977, p. 2.

[75] *Sovetskaya Litva,* June 29, 1977, p. 1. For other letters agreeing with the engineer's emphasis, see also *Bakinskiy Rabochiy,* June 28, 1977, p. 2.; *Izvestiya,* July 7, 1977, p. 2; and *Pravda,* July 17, 1977, p. 3. For letters advocating increased "moral" incentives, see, e.g., *Sovetskaya Litva,* June 28, 1977, p. 2; *Izvestiya,* July 12, 1977, p. 2; *Vechernyaya Moskva,* July 30, 1977, p. 2; and *Krasnaya zvezda,* August 16, 1977, p. 2.

[76] For the comment of the Moscow factory worker, see *Vechernyaya Moskva,* July 16, 1977, p. 2. For letters proposing legal sanctions, see, e.g., *Literaturnaya gazeta,* No. 27, July 6, 1977, p. 2; *Komsomol'skaya pravda,* July 23, 1977, p. 2; and *Pravda,* August 1, 1977, p. 3. See the proposal on anti-parasitism by Deputy A.V. Ivanov at the first session of the newly-elected Leningrad City Soviet, *Izvestiya,* June 25, 1977, p. 3. See also *Pravda Ukrainy,* July 1, 1977, p. 2; *Sovetskaya Litva,* July 7, 1977, p. 2; *Pravda,* July 12, 1977, p. 3; *ibid.,* July 13, 1977, p. 3; *ibid.,* August 3, 1977, p. 3; *Vechernyaya Moskva,* August 10, 1977, p. 2; and *Pravda,* September 9, 1977, p. 3.

[77] *Pravda,* July 8, 1977, p. 3; and *Vechernyaya Moskva,* July 9, 1977, p. 2. See also, *Pravda,* September 8, 1977, p. 3.

[78] *Vechernyaya Moskva,* July 7, 1977, p. 2; *Izvestiya,* July 9, 1977, p. 2; and *Komsomol'skaya pravda,* July 22, 1977, p. 1. See also, *Vechernyaya Moskva,* August 17, 1977, p. 2; and *Pravda,* August 21, 1977, p. 3.

[79] *Izvestiya,* July 7, 1977, p. 2; *ibid.,* June 30, 1977, p. 2; and *ibid.,* July 2, 1977, p. 2. See also, *Pravda,* September 14, 1977, p. 3.

[80] *Izvestiya,* June 28, 1977, p. 2; *ibid.,* July 9, 1977, p. 2; and *Pravda,* July 9, 1977, p. 3. See also, *Izvestiya,* July 14, 1977, p. 2; *Pravda,* August 14, 1977, p. 3; and *ibid.,* September 9, 1977, p. 3. A related participatory clause, Art. 96 which conferred the "right . . . to be elected" Deputies on 18-year-olds, stirred considerable discussion pro and con. See, e.g., *Pravda,* September 18, 1977, p. 3. The result in the final, amended text was a compromise.

[81] *Izvestiya,* July 15, 1977, p. 2; *Sovetskaya Litva,* July 3, 1977, p. 2.

[82] *Izvestiya,* July 16, 1977, p. 2; *Komsomol'skaya pravda,* July 22, 1977, p. 1; and *Vechernyaya Moskva,* July 22, 1977, p. 2. See also *Pravda Ukrainy,* July 3, 1977, p. 2; and *Pravda,* August 1, 1977, p. 3.

[83] *Izvestiya,* July 7, 1977, p. 2; *Pravda,* July 3, 1977, p. 3; *Pravda Ukrainy,* June 29, 1977, p. 1. See also *Pravda,* June 27, 1977, p. 3; *Pravda's* lead editorial, July 3, 1977, p. 1; *Izvestiya,* August 6, 1977, p. 2; *Pravda,* August 23, 1977, p. 3; and *Izvestiya,* September 9, 1977, p. 2. The absence of reference to these two institutions in the Draft Constitution was apparently not meant to signal their gradual "withering away." In a May 1977 speech, USSR Minister of Justice V.I. Terebilov indicated that both institutions

have been given increased authority and responsibility in order to fulfill their assigned roles in the implementation of the new legislation on juvenile delinquency, enacted in February 1977. See *Pravda*, May 20, 1977, p. 3, as translated in *CDSP*, June 15, 1977, pp. 1-2. For basic studies on these institutions, see Harold J. Berman and James Spindler, "Soviet Comrades' Courts," *Washington Law Review*, Vol. 38, 1963, pp. 842-910; and Dennis M. O'Connor, "Soviet People's Guards: An Experiment with Civic Police," *New York University Law Review*, Vol. 39, 1964, pp. 579-614.

[84]*Pravda*, July 15, 1977, pp. 2-3; *Vechernyaya Moskva*, June 28, 1977, p. 2; and *Izvestiya*, July 13, 1977, p. 2. See also *ibid.*, August 6, 1977, p. 2; and *Vechernyaya Moskva*, August 10, 1977, p. 2.

[85]*Pravda*, July 8, 1977, p. 3; *Krasnaya zvezda*, July 23, 1977, p. 2; and *Izvestiya*, July 24, 1977, p. 2. See also *Pravda*, July 28, 1977, p. 3. For a readers' "debate" on the personal property clause (Art. 13), see *ibid.*, July 30, 1977, p. 3.

[86]*Vechernyaya Moskva*, June 21, 1977, p. 2; *ibid.*, July 11, 1977, p. 2 (two letters); *ibid.*, August 22, 1977, p. 2; *Komsomol'skaya pravda*, July 31, 1977, p. 1; and *Izvestiya*, August 6, 1977, p. 2.

[87]See, e.g., the attacks on Zbigniew Brzezinski in *Komsomol'skaya pravda*, May 25, 1977, p. 3, as translated in *CDSP*, June 22, 1977, pp. 6-7, and on President Carter in *Izvestiya*, June 9, 1977, p. 5. Later in the summer, the polomics shifted from personalities and policies to the U.S. system as a whole. See, e.g., the extended comparative critique of the U.S. Constitution in *Literaturnaya gazeta*, No. 35, August 31, 1977, p. 13.

[88]*Pravda*, July 8, 1977, p. 3; *ibid.*, July 16, 1977, p. 3; and *Sovetskaya Litva*, July 8, 1977, p. 2. See also *Pravda Ukrainy*, July 1, 1977, p. 2. Brezhnev had given some emphasis in his Report to the linkage of rights and duties, and the press cued the public on this issue rather heavily in lead editorials. See *Vechernyaya Moskva*, June 6, 1977, p. 1; *Izvestiya*, June 8, 1977, p. 1; and *Krasnaya zvezda*, June 21, 1977, p. 1.

[89]*Izvestiya*, July 3, 1977, p. 2; *Pravda Ukrainy*, July 8, 1977, p. 2; and *Pravda*, July 14, 1977, p. 3. See also *Izvestiya*, August 18, 1977, p. 2.

[90]On Sakharov's appeal, see *Le Monde* (Paris), June 4, 1977, p. 5. For his subsequent statement, see *The New York Times*, June 6, 1977, p. 4. See also G. Snigerev's "Open Letter to the Soviet Government," *Russkaya mysl'* (Paris), July 7, 1977, p. 2. He argued that the "linkage" of rights with duties (Art. 39), combined with the caveat of Art. 50, effectively "canceled" his rights as a citizen. Snigerev is a writer and documentary film maker who had been active in Ukrainian dissident circles since 1966. In 1974 he was expelled from membership in the Communist Party and the professional organization necessary for him to work in films, apparently for refusing to renounce publicly his friendship with the dissident writer Viktor

Nekrasov, now an émigré. For information on dissidents' reactions to the Soviet Draft Constitution, I am indebted to Dr. Gene Sosin, Radio Free Europe/Radio Liberty, New York, New York. For post-ratification émigré dissident criticism of the new Soviet Constitution in general and its civil rights clauses in particular, see Vladimir Bukovsky, "An Appeal to the Heads of State and Government of the Thirty-five Countries that Signed the Helsinki Agreements," *New York Review of Books,* October 13, 1977, p. 44; and Valery Chalidze, "Human Rights in the New Soviet Constitution," *A Chronicle of Human Rights in the USSR,* No. 28, October-December 1977.

[91]Article 52 reads in part: "The incitement of hostility and hatred in connection with religious beliefs is prohibited."

[92]Information on the religious appeal is from RFE/RL. For the party rule referred to in the religious petition, see John N. Hazard, *The Soviet System of Government,* 4th ed. (Chicago: University of Chicago Press, 1968), Appendix, p. 244. In contrast to the religious dissidents, a colonel in the military law office of the Soviet Army urged a far more restrictive religious freedom clause (Art. 52). See *Krasnaya zvezda,* July 31, 1977, p. 2. See also, *Pravda,* September 1, 1977, p. 3.

[93]*Bakinskiy rabochiy,* July 2, 1977, p. 2; and *Literaturnaya gazeta,* No. 29, July 20, 1977, p. 2. See also *Izvestiya,* August 17, 1977, p. 2.

[94]Article 155 specifies that both "Judges and people's assessors are independent and subordinate only to the law."

[95]Doctor of Jurisprudence G.Z. Anashkin is former Chairman of the Criminal Division of the USSR Supreme Court. His article appeared in *Pravda,* July 11, 1977, p. 3. Also see *Izvestiya,* July 3, 1977, p. 2; *Pravda,* July 8, 1977, p. 3; and the joint letter from two well-known jurists urging reinforcement of the independence of the procurator from the local soviet in his jurisdiction, as a safeguard for ensuring the observance of legality, *Izvestiya,* August 3, 1977, p. 2. Earlier, in *samizdat,* Roy Medvedev had advanced similar proposals. He, too, suggested broadening the court's jurisdiction so that citizens could seek judicial remedies against administrative abuses. See his *On Socialist Democracy* (New York: Knopf, 1975), esp. pp. 162-63. On the policy and law of pardon, see Zigurds L. Zile, "Amnesty and Pardon in the Soviet Union," *Soviet Union,* Vol. 3, Part 1, 1976, pp. 37-49.

[96]*Pravda,* July 6, 1977, p. 3.

[97]Deputy Procurator Gusev was far less persuasive in his previous "exchange" with Sakharov and Chalidze on the Op-Ed Page of *The New York Times.* See *The New York Times,* February 23, 1977, p. A23; Valery Chalidze's rebuttal, March 5, 1977, p. 19; and Sakharov's reply, March 29, 1977, p. 27.

[98]*Pravda,* July 11, 1977, p. 3; *Izvestiya,* July 3, 1977, p. 2; and Snigerev, "Open Letter." Snigerev was referring to the conviction of two Ukrainian dissidents in June 1977 for their leadership of an unofficial "watch group" in Kiev whose purpose was to monitor Soviet compliance with the Helsinki accords. The trial had taken place in an out-of-the-way small town instead of in Kiev, thus making it very difficult for the defendants' relatives and supporters to attend and in effect rendering it *de facto* a "closed trial." A few months later, in September 1977, Snigerev was arrested in Kiev. See *A Chronicle of Human Rights in the USSR,* No. 27, July-September 1977, p. 21.

[99]*Izvestiya,* July 3, 1977, p. 2; *ibid.,* June 26, 1977, p. 2; and *Pravda,* August 3, 1977, p. 3. On the earlier debates over the right to counsel and the presumption of innocence, see Gorgone, "Soviet Jurists in the Legislative Arena: The Reform of Criminal Procedure, 1956-1958," *loc. cit.;* and Kazimierz Grzybowski, "Soviet Criminal Law," *Problems of Communism,* March-April 1965, especially pp. 60-62.

[100]While everyone may be "for" science, this does not preclude possibly serious disputes over the allocation of science-targeted funds. In particular, those who would tighten the "link with production" by directing a still larger share of the science budget into "applied research" will no doubt come into conflict with the interests supporting "basic research."

[101]For a sample of such letters, see *Pravda,* June 27, 1977, p. 3; *ibid.,* July 20, 1977, p. 3; *ibid.,* August 3, 1977, p. 3; *ibid.,* August 14, 1977, p. 3; *Izvestiya,* July 1, 1977, p. 2; *ibid.,* August 3, 1977, p. 2; *Vechernyaya Moskva,* July 7, 1977, p. 2; and *Bakinskiy rabochiy,* July 1, 1977, p. 2. See also, *Pravda,* September 14, 1977, p. 3.

[102]*Pravda,* July 10, 1977, p. 3; *Izvestiya,* July 8, 1977, p. 2; *Pravda,* July 21, 1977, p. 3; and *Vechernyaya Moskva,* June 27, 1977, p. 2. The enactment in June 1977 by the USSR Supreme Soviet of the all-union Fundamental Principles of Forest Legislation, which was accompanied by a number of pro-environmentalist speeches by various deputies, gave additional impetus, no doubt, to the *ad hoc* lobby on environmentalism. See *Izvestiya,* June 18, 1977, pp. 1-7. For other letters on the general issue, see, e.g., *Bakinskiy Rabochiy,* July 1, 1977, p. 2; *Ekonomicheskaya gazeta,* No. 27, July 1977, p. 8; *ibid.,* No. 30, July 1977, p. 6; *Izvestiya,* July 24, 1977, p. 2; *Krasnaya zvezda,* July 30, 1977, p. 2; *Pravda,* August 22, 1977, p. 3; and *ibid.,* September 11, 1977, p. 3.

[103]See *CDSP,* October 26, 1977, p. 4. According to well-informed sources with whom the author has had discussions, the enlarged Secretariat numbered approximately 500 people and the two articles which drew the most communications were reportedly the housing clause (Art. 44) and the clause on "individual labor activity" (Art. 17). Apparently, thousands of people took advantage of the public discussion on the new right of housing

to write to higher authorities complaining about and seeking improvements in their housing arrangements.

[104]For a translation of Brezhnev's fall report on the proposed constitutional revisions, see *CDSP,* October 26, 1977, pp. 1-7 and 13, esp. pp. 1 and 5. The final text of the 1977 Constitution was published in *Pravda* and other major newspapers on October 8, 1977. For an English translation, see *CDSP,* November 9, 1977, pp. 1-13, reprinted in this volume at p. 73. Beginning in 1977, October 7 replaced December 5 as Soviet "Constitution Day."

[105]See *CDSP, ibid.,* p. 2, reprinted in the present volume at p. 76.

[106]Otto Kirchheimer, "The *Rechtsstaat* as Magic Wall," in Kurt H. Wolff and Barrington Moore, Jr., eds. *The Critical Spirit, Essays in Honor of Herbert Marcuse* (Boston: Beacon Press, 1967), p. 312.

THE NEW SOVIET CONSTITUTION OF 1977: OFFICIAL TEXT

The Great October Socialist Revolution, carried out by the workers and peasants of Russia under the leadership of the Communist Party headed by V. I. Lenin, overthrew the power of the capitalists and landowners, broke the fetters of oppression, *established the dictatorship of the proletariat** and created the Soviet state — a new type of state and the basic instrument for the defense of revolutionary gains and the construction of socialism and communism. *Mankind's world-historic turn from capitalism to socialism began.*

---

*Additions to the draft version and new wordings are indicated by *italic type*. Deletions from the draft and old wordings are enclosed in brackets [ ]. Footnotes explain some more lengthy and complicated changes and appear at the end of the Constitution.

After winning victory in the Civil War and repulsing imperialist intervention, Soviet power carried out profound social and economic transformations and once and for all ended the exploitation of man by man, class antagonisms and national enmity. *The unification of the Soviet republics in the USSR multiplied the forces and possibilities of the country's peoples in the construction of socialism.* Public ownership of the means of production and genuine democracy for the masses of working people were established. For the first time in the history of mankind, a socialist society has been created.

The unfading exploit of the Soviet people and their Armed Forces in winning the historic victory in the Great Patriotic War was a brilliant manifestation of the strength of socialism. This victory strengthened the *prestige and* international position of the USSR and opened up new and favorable possibilities for the growth of the forces of socialism, national liberation, democracy and peace the world over.

Continuing their creative activity, *the working people of the Soviet Union* [Soviet people] have ensured the country's rapid and comprehensive development and the improvement of the socialist system. The alliance of the working class, the collective farm peasantry and the people's intelligentsia and the friendship of the USSR's nations and nationalities have been consolidated. Social, political *and ideological* unity has come about in Soviet society, in which the working class is the leading force. Having fulfilled the tasks of the dictatorship of the proletariat, the Soviet state has become a state of all the people. The leading role of the Communist Party — the vanguard of all the people — has grown.

A developed socialist society has been built in the USSR. At this stage, when socialism is developing on its own foundation, the creative forces of the new system and the advantages of the socialist way of life are being disclosed more and more fully, and the working people are making ever wider use of the fruits of the great revolutionary gains.

This is a society in which mighty productive forces and advanced science and culture have been created, in which the people's well-being is growing steadily and increasingly favorable conditions for the all-round development of the individual are taking shape.

This is a society of mature socialist social relations, in which a new historical community of people — the Soviet people — has come into being on the basis of the drawing together of all *classes and* social strata and the juridical and actual equality of all nations and nationalities *and their fraternal cooperation.*

This is a society in which the working people — patriots and internationalists — have a high degree of organization, ideological conviction and class consciousness.

This is a society in which the law of life is the concern of all for the *welfare* [well-being] of each and the concern of each for the *welfare* [well-being] of all.

This is a society of genuine democracy, whose political system ensures the effective administration of all public affairs, the increasingly active participation of the working people in state life and the combination of real *citizens'* [human] rights and liberties with *their duties and responsibility to society* [civic responsibility].

The developed socialist society is a logically necessary stage on the path to communism.

The supreme goal of the Soviet state is the building of a

classless communist society *in which public communist self-government will receive development*. The principal tasks of the *socialist* state *of all the people* are: creating the material and technical base of communism, improving socialist social relations and transforming them into communist relations, rearing the man of communist society, raising the working people's material and cultural living standard, safeguarding the country's security and helping to strengthen peace and to develop international cooperation.

The Soviet people,

guided by the ideas of scientific communism and maintaining fidelity to their revolutionary traditions,

relying on the great social, economic and political gains of socialism,

striving for the further development of socialist democracy,

taking into account the international position of the USSR as a component part of the world socialist system, and conscious of their international responsibility,

preserving the continuity of the ideas and principles of the *first*, 1918 *Soviet* [RSFSR] Constitution, the 1924 USSR Constitution and the 1936 USSR Constitution,

formalize the principles of the USSR's social system and policy, establish the rights, liberties and duties of citizens and the principles of organization and aims of the socialist state of all the people, and proclaim them in this Constitution.[1]

I. PRINCIPLES OF THE SOCIAL (SOCIOPOLITICAL AND ECONOMIC) SYSTEM AND POLICY OF THE USSR.

Chapter 1.
THE POLITICAL SYSTEM.

Article 1.—The Union of Soviet Socialist Republics is a socialist state of all the people, expressing the will and interests of the *workers* [working class], *peasants* [the peasantry] and the intelligentsia and of *the working people of* all the country's nations and nationalities.

Article 2.—All power in the USSR belongs to the people.

The people exercise state power through the Soviets of People's Deputies, which constitute the political foundation of the USSR.

All other state agencies are under the control of and accountable to the Soviets *of People's Deputies.*

Article 3.—The organization and activity of the Soviet state are constructed in accordance with the principle of democratic centralism: the elective nature of all bodies of state power, from top to bottom, their accountability to the people, and the binding nature of the decisions of higher bodies on lower. Democratic centralism combines single leadership with local initiative and creative activeness, with the responsibility of every state agency and official for the assigned task.

Article 4.—The Soviet state and all its agencies operate on the basis of socialist legality and ensure the protection of law and order, the interests of society and the rights *and liberties* of citizens.

State [institutions] and public organizations and officials

are obliged to observe the USSR Constitution and Soviet laws.

Article 5.—The most important questions of state life are submitted for nationwide discussion and are also put up for a nationwide vote (referendum).

Article 6.—The Communist Party of the Soviet Union is the leading and guiding force of Soviet society, the nucleus of its political system and of [all] state and public organizations. The CPSU exists for the people and serves the people.

Armed with the Marxist-Leninist teaching, the Communist Party determines general prospects for the development of society and the lines of the USSR's domestic and foreign policy, directs the great creative activity of the Soviet people, and gives their struggle for the victory of communism a planned, scientifically substantiated nature.

All Party organizations operate within the framework of the USSR Constitution.

Article 7.—In accordance with their statutory tasks, trade unions, the All-Union Lenin Young Communist League and cooperative and other [mass] public organizations participate in the administration of state and public affairs and in the resolution of political, economic, social and cultural questions.

Article 8.—*Labor collectives participate in the discussion and resolution of state and public affairs, in the planning of production and social development, in the training and placement of cadres, and in the discussion and resolution of questions of the management of enterprises and institutions, the improvement of working and living conditions, and the use of funds earmarked for the development of production and for social and cultural measures and material incentives.*

Labor collectives develop socialist competition, facilitate the dissemination of advanced methods of work and the strengthening of labor discipline, instill in their members a spirit of communist morality, and show concern for increasing their political consciousness, raising their cultural level and improving their occupational quali- fications.[2]

Article 9 [Article 8 in the draft].—The basic direction of the development of the political system of Soviet society is the further unfolding of socialist democracy: the ever wider participation of *citizens* [the working people] in the administration of the affairs of the state and of society, the improvement of the state apparatus, an increase in the activeness of public organizations, the intensification of people's control, the strengthening of the legal foundations of state and public life, greater publicity, and constant consideration for public opinion.

Chapter 2.
THE ECONOMIC SYSTEM.

Article 10 [Article 9].—Socialist ownership of the means of production, in the form of state ownership (that of all the people) and collective farm-cooperative ownership [and ownership by trade union and other public organizations], is the foundation of the USSR's economic system.

Socialist ownership also extends to the property of trade union and other public organizations needed to carry out their statutory tasks.[3]

The state protects socialist property and creates condi- tions for its multiplication.

No one has the right to use socialist property for purposes of personal gain *or for other selfish purposes.*

Article 11 [Article 10].—State ownership — the common property of all the Soviet people — is the principal form of socialist ownership.

The land, its mineral wealth, the waters and the forests are the exclusive property of the state. The principal means of production in industry, construction and agriculture, means of transport and communication, banks, *the property of* trade, *municipal-service and other* [social and consumer-service] enterprises *organized by the state* and the bulk of the urban housing stock, *as well as other property necessary to carry out the state's tasks,* belong to the state.

Article 12 [Article 11].—The property of collective farms and other cooperative organizations and of their associations is the means of production and other property *necessary for* [that serves] the implementation of their statutory tasks.

The land occupied by collective farms is assigned to them for free use for an unlimited time.

The state assists the development of collective farm-cooperative ownership and its approximation to state ownership.

The collective farms, like other land users, are obliged to use land effectively, take a solicitous attitude toward it and increase its fertility.

Article 13 [Article 12].—*Earned income constitutes the foundation of the personal property of USSR citizens. Personal property may include* [USSR citizens may have in their personal possession] household articles, articles of personal consumption and convenience, *articles needed for auxiliary household farming operations,* a house and earned [income and] savings [and an auxiliary farming operation]. The personal property of citizens and their right to its inheritance are protected by *the state* [law].

Citizens may have the use of plots of land made available [by the state or by the collective farms], under a procedure established by law, for auxiliary farming operations (including the keeping of livestock and poultry), the growing of fruit and vegetables, and also for individual housing construction. *Citizens are obliged to make rational use of the plots of land made available to them. The state and the collective farms provide assistance to citizens in auxiliary farming operations.*

Property in the personal possession or use of citizens may not serve for the derivation of unearned income or be used to harm *the interests of* society.

Article 14 [Article 13].—The [free] labor of Soviet people, *free from exploitation,* is the source of the growth of social wealth and of the well-being of the people and of every Soviet person.

The state exercises control over the measure of labor and consumption in accordance with the principle *of socialism*: "From each according to his ability, to each according to his work." It determines the size of the income tax *on taxable income* [and establishes the level of wages exempted from the payment of taxes].

Socially useful labor and its results determine the status of a person in society. By combining material and moral incentives *and encouraging innovation and a creative attitude toward work*, the state helps turn labor into a prime necessity in the life of every Soviet person.

Article 15 [Article 14].—The highest goal of social production under socialism is the fullest possible satisfaction of people's growing material and spiritual requirements.

Relying on the creative activeness of the working people, socialist competition and the achievements of scientific and technical progress *and improving the forms and methods of economic management,* the state ensures the growth of labor productivity, increases in production efficiency and the quality of work, and the dynamic, *planned* and proportional development of the national economy.

Article 16 [Article 15].—The economy of the USSR is a single national-economic complex embracing all elements of social production, distribution and exchange on the country's territory.

Management of the economy is carried out on the basis of state plans *of economic and social development* [for the development of the national economy and social and cultural construction], taking branch and territorial principles into account, and combining centralized management with the economic independence and initiative of enterprises, associations and other organizations. In this process, active use is made of economic accountability, profit, unit cost *and other economic levers and incentives.*

Article 17.—Individual labor activity in the sphere of handicrafts, agriculture and consumer services for the population, as well as other types of activity based exclusively on the personal labor of citizens and members of their families, is permitted in the USSR in accordance with the law. *The state regulates individual labor activity, seeing to it that it is used in the interests of society.*

Article 18.—In the interests of present and future generations, the necessary steps are being taken in the USSR to protect and make scientifically substantiated and rational use of the land and its mineral wealth, *water resources* and flora and fauna, to preserve the purity of the air and water, to ensure the reproduction of natural resources, and to improve man's environment.

Chapter 3.
SOCIAL DEVELOPMENT AND CULTURE.

Article 19.—*The social foundation of the USSR is the indestructible alliance of workers, peasants and the intelligentsia.*

The [Soviet] state helps in increasing the social homogeneity of society — in effacing the class differences between city and countryside and between mental and physical labor and in the *all-round* [continued] development and drawing together of all the USSR's nations and nationalities.

Article 20.—In accordance with the communist ideal, "The free development of each is the condition for the free development of all," the [Soviet] state has as its goal the expansion of real possibilities for the [development and] application of the creative forces, abilities and talents of citizens and for the all-round development of individuals.

Article 21.—The state shows concern for the improvement of working conditions *and labor protection, for the scientific organization of labor* and for the reduction and, eventually, the complete elimination of arduous *physical* [manual] labor on the basis of the comprehensive mechanization and automation of production *processes in all branches of the national economy.*

Article 22.—The USSR consistently implements a program of the transformation of agricultural labor into a variety of industrial labor; the expansion in rural localities of the network of public education, culture, public health, trade, *public catering, consumer-service* and municipal-service institutions; and the transformation of villages into well-appointed settlements.

Article 23.—*On the basis of* [In accordance with] the growth of labor productivity, the state steadfastly pursues a course aimed at raising the level of remuneration for labor and the real incomes of the working people.

Public consumption funds are created for the purpose of the fuller satisfaction of the requirements of *Soviet people* [members of society]. The state, with the broad participation of public organizations and labor collectives, ensures the growth and fair distribution of these funds.

Article 24.—State systems of public health, social insurance, *trade,* public catering, consumer services and municipal services operate and are developing in the USSR.

The state encourages the activity of cooperative and other public organizations in *all spheres* [the field] of services to the population. *It promotes the development of mass physical culture and sports.*

Article 25.—A unified system of public education exists *and is being improved* in the USSR; it *ensures the general-education and vocational training of citizens,* serves the communist up-bringing and the spiritual and physical development of young people, and prepares them for labor and public activity. [Education in the USSR is free.]

Article 26.—In accordance with the requirements of society, the state ensures the planned development of science and the training of scientific cadres, and it organizes the introduction of the results of scientific research in the national economy and other spheres of life.

Article 27.—The state shows concern for the protection, multiplication and broad utilization of [society's] spiritual values for *the moral and aesthetic upbringing of* Soviet people and for raising their cultural level.

The development of professional art and amateur artistic activity is given every encouragement in the USSR.

Chapter 4.
FOREIGN POLICY.

Article 28.—The *USSR* [Soviet state] *steadfastly* [consistently] pursues a Leninist policy of peace, and it stands for the consolidation of the security of peoples and broad international cooperation.

The USSR's foreign policy is aimed at ensuring favorable international conditions for building communism in the USSR, *protecting the Soviet Union's state interests,* strengthening the positions of world socialism, supporting the peoples' struggle for national liberation and social progress, preventing wars of aggression, *achieving general and complete disarmament* and consistently implementing the principle of the peaceful coexistence of states with different social systems.

In the USSR, war propaganda is forbidden [by law].

Article 29.—The USSR's relations with other states are constructed on the basis of observance of the principles of sovereign equality; mutual renunciation of the use of force or the threat of force; the inviolability of borders; the territorial integrity of states; the peaceful settlement of disputes; noninterference in internal affairs; respect for human rights and basic liberties; equality and the right of peoples to decide their own fate; cooperation between states; and the conscientious fulfillment of commitments stemming from generally recognized principles and norms of international law and from international treaties concluded by the USSR.

Article 30.—The *USSR* [Soviet Union], as a component part of the world socialist system and the socialist common-wealth, develops and strengthens friendship, cooperation and comradely mutual assistance with other socialist countries on the basis of *the principle of* socialist internationalism and actively participates in economic integration and in the international socialist division of labor.

Chapter 5.
DEFENSE OF THE SOCIALIST FATHERLAND.

Article 31.—Defense of the socialist fatherland is one of the most important functions of the state and is the affair of all the people.

For the purpose of defending socialist gains, the peaceful labor of the Soviet people and the sovereignty and territorial integrity of the state, the USSR Armed Forces have been created and universal military service has been established.

The USSR Armed Forces' duty to the people is to reliably defend the socialist fatherland and to maintain constant combat readiness, guaranteeing an immediate rebuff to any aggressor.

Article 32.—The state ensures the country's security and defense capability and outfits the USSR Armed Forces with everything they need.

The obligations of state agencies, public organizations, officials and citizens in ensuring the country's security and strengthening its defense capability are defined by *USSR legislation* [law].

II. THE STATE AND THE INDIVIDUAL.

Chapter 6.
USSR CITIZENSHIP.
THE EQUALITY OF CITIZENS.

Article 33.—Uniform Union citizenship is established in the USSR. Every citizen of a Union republic is a USSR citizen.

The grounds and procedure for acquiring and losing Soviet citizenship are *defined* [established] by *the Law on USSR Citizenship* [USSR law].

USSR citizens abroad enjoy the protection of the Soviet state.

Article 34.—USSR citizens are equal before the law, regardless of origin, social or property status, race or nationality, sex, education, language, attitude to religion, nature or type of employment, place of residence or other circumstances.

Equal rights for USSR citizens are ensured in all fields of economic, political, social and cultural life.

Article 35.—Women and men have equal rights in the USSR.

The exercise of these rights is ensured by providing women with opportunities equal *to those of men* in receiving an education and vocational training, in labor, remuneration and promotion and in social, political and cultural activity, as well as by special measures to protect women's labor and health; *by the creation of conditions enabling women to combine labor and motherhood;* by legal protection and material and moral support for mother and child, including the granting of paid leave and other benefits to pregnant women and mothers; and by *the gradual reduction of working time for women with small children* [state aid to single mothers].

Article 36.—*USSR* [Soviet] citizens of different races and nationalities have equal rights.

The exercise of these rights is ensured by the policy of the all-round development and drawing together of all the USSR's nations and nationalities, the fostering in citizens of a spirit of Soviet patriotism and socialist internationalism, and the opportunity to use the mother tongue and languages of other peoples of the USSR.

Any kind of direct or indirect restriction of the rights of citizens or the establishment of any direct or indirect advantages for citizens on a racial or national basis, as well as any preaching of racial or national exclusiveness, hostility or contempt, is punishable by law.

Article 37.—Foreign citizens and stateless persons in the USSR are guaranteed the rights and liberties provided by law, including the right to institute proceedings in courts and other state agencies for the protection of personal, property, family or other rights belonging to them [by law].

While on USSR territory, foreign citizens and stateless persons are obliged to respect the USSR Constitution and to observe Soviet laws.

Article 38.—The USSR affords the right of asylum to foreigners who are persecuted for defending the interests of the working people and the cause of peace, for participating in a revolutionary or national-liberation movement, or for progressive sociopolitical, scientific or other creative activity.

Chapter 7.
THE BASIC RIGHTS, LIBERTIES AND DUTIES OF USSR CITIZENS.

Article 39.—USSR citizens possess the whole range of social, economic, political and personal rights and liberties proclaimed in and guaranteed by the USSR Constitution and Soviet laws. The socialist system ensures the expansion of rights and liberties and the continuous improvement of the living conditions of citizens in step with the fulfillment of programs of social, economic and cultural development.

The exercise of rights and liberties by citizens must not injure the interests of society and the state or the rights of other citizens.

Article 40.—USSR citizens have the right to labor — that is, to receive guaranteed work and remuneration for labor in accordance with its quantity and quality *and not below the minimum amount established by the state* — including the right to choice of occupation, type of employment and work in accordance with one's primary vocation, capabilities, vocational training and education and with consideration for social requirements.

This right is ensured by the socialist economic system, the steady growth of productive forces [of society], free vocational instruction, the improvement of labor skills and training in new specialties, *and the development of the systems of vocational guidance and job placement.*

Article 41.—USSR citizens have the right to rest.

This right is ensured by the *establishment of a* [41-hour] workweek *not exceeding 41 hours* for workers and office employees, a shortened working day for a number of occupations and production sectors, and shorter working hours at night; the provision of annual paid vacations and weekly days off, and also by the expansion of the network of cultural-enlightenment and health-improvement institutions and the large-scale development of sports, physical culture and tourism; and the creation of favorable opportunities for rest at one's place of residence and other conditions for the rational use of free time.

The length of working time and of rest for collective farmers is regulated by the collective *farms* [farm charters].

Article 42.—USSR citizens have the right to health care.

This right is ensured by free and qualified medical assistance, provided by state public health institutions; by the expansion of the network of institutions for providing citizens with medical treatment and health-improvement services; by the development and improvement of safety measures and industrial sanitation; by conducting wide-scale preventive-medicine measures; by measures to improve the environment; by special concern for the health of the growing generation, including the prohibition of child labor *not involving training and labor upbringing;* and by the development of scientific research aimed at preventing disease, reducing its incidence and ensuring long and active lives for citizens.

Article 43.—USSR citizens have the right to material security in old age, in case of illness, and in the event of complete or partial disability or loss of breadwinner.

This right is guaranteed by social insurance for workers, office employees and collective farmers and by temporary disability allowances; by *the payment by the state and by collective farms of* old-age and disability pensions and pensions for loss of breadwinner; by the job placement of citizens with partial disability; by care for [single] elderly citizens and for invalids; *and by other forms of social insurance.*

Article 44.—USSR citizens have the right to housing.

This right is ensured by the development and protection of the state and public housing stock, by assistance to cooperative and individual housing construction, by the fair distribution, under public control, of housing space allotted in accordance with the implementation of the program for the construction of *well-appointed* housing, and also by low apartment rents *and charges for municipal services. USSR citizens must take good care of the housing allocated to them.*

Article 45.—USSR citizens have the right to education.

This right is ensured by the free nature of all types of education, the implementation of the universal compulsory secondary education of young people and the broad development of vocational-technical, specialized secondary and higher education based on the linkage of instruction with life and production; by the development of correspondence and evening education; by the provision of state stipends and other benefits for pupils and students; by the free issuance of school textbooks; by the opportunity for school instruction in one's native tongue; and by the [development of the vocational guidance system and the] creation of conditions for [the working people's] self-education.

Article 46.—USSR citizens have the right to use cultural achievements.

This right is ensured by general access to the values of Soviet and world culture in state and public collections; by the development and balanced distribution of cultural-enlightenment institutions in the country; *by the development of television, radio, book publishing, the periodical press and the network of free libraries;* and by the expansion of cultural exchanges with foreign states.

Article 47.—USSR citizens, in accordance with the goals of communist construction, are guaranteed freedom of scientific, technical and artistic creation. This freedom is ensured by the extensive development of scientific research, invention and rationalization activity and by the development of *literature and* the arts. The state creates the necessary material conditions for this, gives support to voluntary societies and unions of creative artists, *and organizes the introduction of inventions and rationalization proposals in the national economy and other spheres of life.*

The rights of authors, inventors and rationalizers are protected by *the state* [law].

Article 48.—USSR citizens have the right to participate in the administration of state and public affairs *and in the discussion and adoption of laws and decisions of nationwide and local importance.*

This right is ensured by the opportunity to elect and be elected to Soviets of People's Deputies and other elective state agencies, to take part in nationwide discussions and votes, in people's control in the work of state agencies, public organizations and public-initiative agencies, and in meetings of labor collectives and meetings at places of residence.[4]

Article 49.—Every USSR citizen has the right to submit to state agencies and public organizations proposals on improving their activity and to criticize shortcomings in work.

Officials are obliged, within the established [by law] time periods, to examine proposals and statements by citizens, to reply to them and to take the necessary steps.

Persecution for criticism is prohibited. *Persons who persecute others for criticism will be called to account.*

Article 50.—In accordance with the [working] people's interests and for the purpose of strengthening *and developing* the socialist system, USSR citizens are guaranteed freedom of speech, of the press, of assembly, of mass meetings and of street processions and demonstrations.

The exercise of these political freedoms is ensured by putting public buildings, streets and squares at the disposal of the working people and their organizations, by the broad dissemination of information, and by the opportunity to use the press, television and radio.

Article 51.—In accordance with the goals of communist construction, USSR citizens have the right to unite in public organizations that facilitate the development of political activeness and initiative and the satisfaction of their diverse interests.

Public organizations are guaranteed conditions for the successful performance of their statutory tasks.

Article 52.—*USSR citizens are guaranteed* freedom of conscience [is recognized for USSR citizens], that is, the right to profess any religion or to profess none, to perform religious worship or to conduct atheistic propaganda. The incitement of hostility and hatred in connection with religious beliefs is prohibited.

In the USSR the church is separate from the state, and the school is separate from the church.

Article 53.—The family is under the protection of the state.

Marriage is *based on* [entered into with] the voluntary agreement of the bride and groom; the spouses are completely equal in family relations.

The state *shows concern for* [aids] the family by creating and developing an extensive network of children's institutions, by organizing and improving consumer services and public catering, by paying childbirth allowances, by providing allowances and benefits for large families, *and by other types of allowances and family assistance.*

Article 54.—USSR citizens are guaranteed inviolability of the person. No one can be arrested except *on the basis of a court decision* [by court order] or with the sanction of a prosecutor.

Article 55.—USSR citizens are guaranteed inviolability of the home. No one has the right, without lawful grounds, to enter a home against the will of the persons living therein.

Article 56.—The private lives of citizens and the confidentiality of correspondence, telephone conversations and telegraph messages are protected by law.

Article 57.—Respect for the individual and the protection of the rights and liberties of *citizens* [Soviet persons] are the obligation of all state agencies, public organizations and officials.

USSR citizens have the right to legal protection against attempts on their honor and dignity, their lives and health, and their personal freedom and property.

Article 58.—USSR citizens have the right to file complaints against the actions of officials and state *and public* agencies [and public organizations]. These complaints are to be examined according to the procedure and within the time periods established by law.

Actions of officials, performed in violation of the law and exceeding their authority, that infringe on the rights of citizens may be protested to a court according to the procedure established by law.

USSR citizens have the right to compensation for damages caused by illegal actions of state [institutions] and public organizations, and also of officials during the performance of their duties [according to the procedure and within the limits established by law].

Article 59.—The exercise of rights and liberties is inseparable from the performance by citizens of their duties.

USSR citizens are obliged to observe the USSR Constitution and Soviet laws, to respect the rules of the socialist community, and to bear with dignity the lofty title of USSR citizen.

Article 60.—Conscientious labor in one's chosen field of socially useful activity and the [strict] observance of labor discipline are the duty of, and a matter of honor for, every able-bodied USSR citizen. *The evasion of socially useful labor is incompatible with the principles of a socialist society.*

Article 61.—The USSR citizen is obliged to protect and enhance socialist property. It is the duty of the USSR citizen to combat the theft and waste of state and public property *and to take good care of the people's property.*

Persons encroaching on socialist property are punishable by law.

Article 62.—The USSR citizen is obliged to safeguard the interests of the Soviet state and to help strengthen its might and prestige.

Defense of the socialist fatherland is the sacred duty of every USSR citizen.

Treason to the homeland is the gravest crime against the people.

Article 63.—Military service in the ranks of the USSR Armed Forces is the honorable duty of Soviet citizens.

Article 64.—It is the duty of every USSR citizen to respect the national dignity of other citizens and to strengthen the friendship of the nations and nationalities of the multinational Soviet state.

Article 65.—The USSR citizen is obliged to respect the rights and legitimate interests of other persons, to be intolerant of antisocial acts, and to assist in every way in the safeguarding of public order.

Article 66.—USSR citizens are obliged to show concern for the upbringing of children, to prepare them for socially useful labor, and to rear worthy members of a socialist society. *Children are obliged to show concern for their parents and to help them.*

Article 67.—USSR citizens are obliged to protect nature and to safeguard its riches.

Article 68 [in the draft, the second paragraph of Article 67].—Concern for the preservation of historical monuments and other cultural values is the duty *and obligation* of USSR citizens.

Article 69 [Article 68].—It is the internationalist duty of the USSR citizen to promote the development of friendship and cooperation with peoples of other countries and the maintenance and strengthening of world peace.

III. THE NATIONAL-STATE STRUCTURE OF THE USSR.

Chapter 8.
THE USSR IS A FEDERAL STATE.
Article 70 [Article 69].—The Union of Soviet Socialist

Republics is a unitary, federal and multinational state, formed *on the basis of the principle of socialist federalism and* as a result of the free self-determination of nations and the voluntary union of equal Soviet Socialist Republics.

The USSR embodies the state unity of the Soviet people and unites all nations and nationalities for the purpose of the joint construction of communism.

Article 71 [Article 70].—The *Union of Soviet Socialist Republics* [USSR] unites:

the Russian Soviet Federated Socialist Republic,
the Ukraine Soviet Socialist Republic,
the Belorussian Soviet Socialist Republic,
the Uzbek Soviet Socialist Republic,
the Kazakh Soviet Socialist Republic,
the Georgian Soviet Socialist Republic,
the Azerbaidzhan Soviet Socialist Republic,
the Lithuanian Soviet Socialist Republic,
the Moldavian Soviet Socialist Republic,
the Latvian Soviet Socialist Republic,
the Kirgiz Soviet Socialist Republic,
the Tadzhik Soviet Socialist Republic,
the Armenian Soviet Socialist Republic
the Turkmenian Soviet Socialist Republic, and
the Estonian Soviet Socialist Republic.

Article 72 [Article 71].—Each Union republic retains the right freely to secede from the USSR.

Article 73 [Article 72].—The jurisdiction of the Union of Soviet Socialist Republics, as represented by its highest bodies of state power and administration, extends to:

(1) the admission of new republics to the USSR; the approval of the formation of new autonomous republics and autonomous provinces within Union republics;

(2) the determination of the USSR's state boundaries and the approval of changes in boundaries between Union republics;

(3) the establishment of general principles for the organization and activity of republic and local bodies of state power and administration;

(4) ensuring the uniformity of legislative regulation throughout the terrritory of the USSR and the establishment of principles of legislation of the USSR and the Union republics;

(5) the implementation of a uniform social and economic policy; the direction of the country's economy; the determination of the basic areas of scientific and technical progress *and of general measures for the rational utilization and conservation of natural resources;* the drafting and approval of *state* plans for the *economic and social development* [development of the national economy and of social and cultural construction] of the USSR and the approval of reports on the fulfillment of such plans;

(6) the drafting and approval of the consolidated USSR State Budget and the approval of the report on its fulfillment; the management of the uniform monetary and credit system; the establishment of taxes and other revenues that go into the formation of *the USSR State Budget* [Union, republic, and local budgets]; the determination of policy in the field of prices and wages;

(7) the direction of branches of the national economy, associations and enterprises of Union subordination; the general direction of branches [associations and enterprises] of Union-republic subordination;

(8) questions of war and peace, the defense of the USSR's sovereignty and the protection of its state borders and

territory, the organization of defense and the direction of the *USSR* Armed Forces;

(9) the safeguarding of state security;

(10) the representation of the USSR in international relations; the USSR's ties with foreign states and international organizations; the establishment of a uniform procedure for and coordination of the Union republics' relations with foreign states and international organizations; foreign trade *and other types of foreign economic activity* on the basis of state monopoly;

(11) control over observance of the USSR Constitution, and ensuring the conformity of Union-republic Constitutions to the USSR Constitution;

(12) the resolution of other questions of all-Union importance.

Article 74 [Article 73].— USSR laws have identical force on the territories of all the Union Republics. In the event of a discrepancy between a Union-republic law and an all-Union law, the USSR law prevails.

Article 75 [Article 74].—The territory of the Union of Soviet Socialist Republics is unitary and comprises the territories of the Union republics.

The sovereignty of the USSR extends to all its territory.

Chapter 9.
THE UNION SOVIET SOCIALIST REPUBLIC.

Article 76 [Article 75].—A Union republic is a *sovereign* Soviet socialist state that has united with other Soviet republics in the Union of Soviet Socialist Republics.

Outside the limits defined in Article *73* [72] of the USSR Constitution, a Union republic independently exercises state power on its territory.

The Union republic has its own Constitution, which conforms to the USSR Constitution and takes the republic's special features into account.

Article 77 [Article 76].—A Union republic participates in the resolution of questions within the jurisdiction of the USSR, doing so in the USSR Supreme Soviet, the Presidium of the USSR Supreme Soviet, the USSR government and other USSR agencies.

A Union republic *ensures comprehensive economic and social development on its territory,* facilitates the exercise of the USSR's authority on its territory, and carries out the decisions of the *highest* USSR bodies of state power and administration.

On questions falling within its jurisdiction, the Union republic coordinates and controls the activity of enterprises, institutions and organizations of Union subordination.

Article 78 [Article 77].—The territory of a Union republic cannot be changed without its consent. The boundaries between Union republics may be changed by mutual agreement of the republics concerned, subject to approval by the USSR.

Article 79 [Article 78].—A Union republic determines its division into territories, provinces, regions and districts and resolves other questions of administrative-territorial structure.

Article 80 [Article 79].—A Union republic has the right to enter into relations with foreign states, to conclude treaties and exchange diplomatic and consular representatives with them, and to participate in the activity of international organizations.

Article 81 [Article 80].—The sovereign rights of the Union republics are protected by the USSR.

Chapter 10.
THE AUTONOMOUS SOVIET SOCIALIST REPUBLIC.

Article 82 [Article 81].—An autonomous republic is part of a Union republic.

Outside the limits of the rights of the USSR and the Union republics, an autonomous republic independently resolves questions falling within it jurisdiction.

An autonomous republic has its own Constitution, which conforms to the USSR Constitution and to the particular Union-republic Constitution and takes the autonomous republic's special features into account.

Article 83 [Article 82].—An autonomous republic participates in the resolution of questions falling within the jurisdiction of the USSR and the particular Union republic, doing so through the highest bodies of state power and administration of the USSR and the Union republic.

An autonomous republic *ensures comprehensive economic and social development on its territory,* facilitates the exercise of the authority of the USSR and the Union republic on its territory, and carries out the decisions of the *highest* USSR and Union-republic bodies of state power and administration.

On questions falling within its jurisdiction, the autonomous republic coordinates and controls the activity of enterprises, institutions and organizations of Union and republic (Union republic) subordination.

Article 84 [Article 83].—The territory of an autonomous republic cannot be changed without its consent.

Article 85 [Article 84].—The Russian Soviet Federated Socialist Republic contains the following autonomous Soviet socialist republics: Bashkir, Buryat, Dagestan,

Kabardino-Balkar, Kalmyk, Karelian, Komi, Mari, Mordvinian, North Ossetian, Tatar, Tuva, Udmurt, Chechen-Ingush, Chuvash, and Yakut.

The Uzbek Soviet Socialist Republic contains the Kara-Kalpak Autonomous Soviet Socialist Republic.

The Georgian Soviet Socialist Republic contains the Abkhaz and Adzhar Autonomous Soviet Socialist Republics.

The Azerbaidzhan Soviet Socialist Republic contains the Nakhichevan Autonomous Soviet Socialist Republic.

Chapter 11.
THE AUTONOMOUS PROVINCE AND THE AUTONOMOUS REGION.

Article 86 [Article 85].—An autonomous province is part of a Union republic *or a territory*. A law on an automonous province is adopted by a Union-republic Supreme Soviet on the basis of a representation submitted by the autonomous province's Soviet of People's Deputies.

Article 87 [Article 86].—The Russian Soviet Federated Socialist Republic contains the following autonomous provinces: Adyge, Gorno-Altai, Jewish, Karachai-Cherkess and Khakass.

The Georgian Soviet Socialist Republic contains the South Ossetian Autonomous Province.

The Azerbaidzhan Soviet Socialist Republic contains the Nagorno-Karabakh Autonomous Province.

The Tadzhik Soviet Socialist Republic contains the Gorno-Badakhshan Autonomous Province.

Article 88 [Article 87].—An autonomous region is part of a territory or province. *Laws* [statutes] on autonomous regions are *adopted* [ratified] by Union-republic Supreme Soviets.

IV. THE SOVIETS OF PEOPLE'S DEPUTIES AND THE PROCEDURE FOR THEIR ELECTION.

Chapter 12.
THE SYSTEM AND PRINCIPLES OF ACTIVITY OF THE SOVIETS OF PEOPLE'S DEPUTIES.

Article 89 [Article 88].—The Soviets of People's Deputies — the USSR Supreme Soviet, the Union-republic Supreme Soviets, the autonomous-republic Supreme Soviets, the territory and province Soviets of People's Deputies, the autonomous-province and autonomous-region Soviets of People's Deputies, the district, city, borough, settlement and rural Soviets of People's Deputies — constitute a unitary system of bodies of state power.

Article 90 [Article 89].—The term of office of the USSR Supreme Soviet, the Union-republic Supreme Soviets and the autonomous-republic Supreme Soviets is five years.

The term of office of *local Soviets of People's Deputies* [the territory and province Soviets of People's Deputies, the autonomous-province and autonomous-region Soviets of People's Deputies and the city, district, borough, settlement and rural Soviets of People's Deputies] is two and a half years.

Elections to Soviets of People's Deputies are set no later than two months before the term of office of the current Soviets expires.

Article 91 [Article 90].—The most important questions within the jurisdiction of the various Soviets of People's Deputies are considered and resolved at their sessions.

The Soviets of People's Deputies elect standing committees and create executive, administrative and other agencies accountable to the Soviets.

Article 92 [Article 91].—The Soviets of People's Deputies form people's control agencies, which combine state control with public control by the working people at enterprises, on collective farms and in institutions and organizations.

The people's control agencies exercise control over the fulfillment of state plans and assignments; combat violations of state discipline, manifestations of parochialism, a departmental approach to matters, mismanagement and wastefulness, red tape and bureaucracy; and help to improve the work of the state apparatus. [The procedure for the organization and activity of the people's control agencies is determined by law.]

Article 93 [Article 92].—The Soviets of People's Deputies, directly or through agencies created by them, direct all branches of state, economic, social and cultural construction, adopt decisions, ensure their fulfillment, and exercise control over the implementation of decisions.

Article 94 [Article 93].—The activity of the Soviets of People's Deputies is constructed on the basis of the collective, free and businesslike discussion and resolution of questions, publicity, regular reporting by executive and administrative agencies and other agencies created by the Soviets to the Soviets and to the population, and the wide-scale enlistment of citizens in the Soviets' work.

Soviets of People's Deputies and the agencies created by them systematically inform the population about their work and the decisions they adopt.

Chapter 13.
THE ELECTORAL SYSTEM.

Article 95 [Article 94].—Elections of Deputies to all Soviets of People's Deputies are conducted on the basis of universal, equal and direct suffrage and by secret ballot.

Article 96 [Article 95].—Elections of Deputies are universal: All USSR citizens who have reached the age of 18 have the right to elect and to be elected, with the exception of persons who have been certified as insane under the procedure established by law.

A USSR citizen who has reached the age of 21 may be elected a Deputy to the USSR Supreme Soviet.

Article 97 [Article 96].—Elections of Deputies are equal: Each elector has one vote; all voters participate in elections on an equal basis.

Article 98 [Article 97].—Elections of Deputies are direct: Deputies to all Soviets of People's Deputies are elected directly by citizens.

Article 99 [Article 98].—Voting in elections for Deputies is secret: Control over the voters' expression of their will is *not permitted* [excluded].

Article 100 [Article 99].—The right to nominate candidates for Deputy belongs to organizations of the Communist Party of the Soviet Union, the trade unions, the All-Union Lenin Young Communist League, cooperative and other public organizations, labor collectives *and meetings of servicemen in their military units.*

USSR citizens and public organizations are guaranteed free and comprehensive discussions of the political, business and personal qualities of candidates for Deputy, as well as the right of campaigning at meetings, in the press and on television and radio.

Expenses connected with the holding of elections to Soviets of People's Deputies are defrayed by the state.

Article 101 [Article 100].—Elections of Deputies to Soviets of People's Deputies are held on the basis of election districts.

A USSR citizen may not, as a rule, be elected to more than two Soviets of People's Deputies.

Elections to Soviets are conducted by electoral commissions, which are made up of representatives of public organizations, labor collectives *and meetings of servicemen in military units.*

The procedure for conducting elections to Soviets of People's Deputies is determined by *USSR, Union-republic and autonomous-republic laws* [law].

Article 102.—*Voters give mandates to their Deputies.*

The appropriate Soviets of People's Deputies examine the voters' mandates, take them into account in drafting plans of economic and social development and in drawing up the budget, organize fulfillment of the mandates, and inform the citizens about their implementation.

Chapter 14.
THE PEOPLE'S DEPUTY.

Article 103 [Article 101].—Deputies are plenipotentiary representatives of the people in the Soviets of People's Deputies.

By participating in the Soviets' work, Deputies resolve questions of state, economic, social and cultural construction, organize the implementation of the Soviets' decisions, and exercise control over the work of state agencies, enterprises, institutions and organizations.

In his activity, the Deputy is guided by state interests,

takes into account the needs of the population of his election district, and seeks to implement the voters' mandates.

Article 104 [Article 102].—The Deputy exercises his authority without terminating his production or service activity.

During the Soviet's sessions, as well as for the exercise of the Deputy's authority in other cases provided by law, the Deputy is released from performing his production or service duties, while retaining his average earnings at his place of permanent employment.

Article 105 [Article 103].—The Deputy has the right to request information from the appropriate state agency or official, who is obliged to respond to the inquiry at a session of the Soviet.

The Deputy is entitled to address inquiries to all state and public agencies, enterprises, institutions and organizations on questions within the scope of the Deputy's activity and to take part in the consideration of questions raised by them. The executives of the state and public agencies, enterprises, institutions and organizations in question are obliged to receive Deputies without delay and to examine their proposals within the *established* time periods [established by law].

Article 106 [Article 104].—The Deputy is provided with conditions for the unhindered and effective exercise of his rights and duties.

The immunity of Deputies, as well as other guarantees of the Deputy's activity, is established by the Law on the Status of Deputies and by other *legislative acts* [legislation] of the USSR and the Union and autonomous republics.

Article 107 [Article 105].—The Deputy is obliged to report on his work and the work of the Soviet to his constituents, *and also to the collectives and public organizations that nominated him as a candidate for Deputy.*

A Deputy who has not justified the trust of his constituents may be recalled at any time by decision of a majority of his constituents, according to the procedure established by law.

V. THE SUPREME BODIES OF STATE POWER AND ADMINISTRATION IN THE USSR.

Chapter 15.
THE USSR SUPREME SOVIET.

Article 108 [Article 106].—The USSR Supreme Soviet is the supreme body of state power in the USSR.

The USSR Supreme Soviet is empowered to resolve all questions placed within the jurisdiction of the USSR by this Constitution.

The adoption of the USSR Constitution and its amendment; the admission of new republics to the USSR and the ratification of the formation of new autonomous republics and autonomous provinces; the ratification of state plans for the *economic and social development of* [development of the national economy and for social and cultural construction in] the USSR, the USSR State Budget and reports on their fulfillment; and the formation of USSR agencies accountable to the USSR Supreme Soviet are exercised exclusively by that body.

USSR laws are adopted [solely] by the USSR Supreme Soviet *or by a nationwide vote (referendum), conducted by decision of the USSR Supreme Soviet.*

Article 109 [Article 107].—The USSR Supreme Soviet consists of two chambers: the Council of the Union and the Council of Nationalities.

The chambers of the USSR Supreme Soviet have equal rights.

Article 110 [Article 108].—The Council of the Union and the Council of Nationalities have an equal number of Deputies.

The Council of the Union is elected on the basis of election districts with equal populations.

The Council of Nationalities is elected according to the following norms: 32 Deputies from each Union republic, 11 Deputies from each autonomous republic, 5 Deputies from each autonomous province and 1 Deputy from each autonomous region.

The Council of the Union and the Council of Nationalities, acting on representations submitted by the credentials committees elected by the councils, adopt decisions on recognizing the credentials of Deputies, and, if there has been a violation of election legislation, on finding the election of individual Deputies invalid.

Article 111 [Article 109].—Each chamber of the USSR Supreme Soviet elects a Chairman of the chamber and four Vice-Chairmen.

The Chairmen of the Council of the Union and the Council of Nationalities preside over the meetings of these chambers and have charge of their proceedings.

Joint [plenary] meetings of the chambers of the USSR Supreme Soviet are presided over alternately by the Chairman of the Council of the Union and the Chairman of the Council of Nationalities.

Article 112 [Article 110].—Sessions of the USSR Supreme Soviet are convened twice a year.

Extraordinary sessions are convened by the Presidium of the USSR Supreme Soviet at its initiative *or on a proposal by a Union republic* or by at least one-third of the Deputies of one of the chambers [and also upon a demand by one of the Union republics].

A session of the USSR Supreme Soviet consists of separate and joint [plenary] meetings of the chambers, and also of meetings of the chambers' standing committees or of the USSR Supreme Soviet's committees held *in the period between the chambers' meetings* [during the session]. A session is open and closed at separate or joint [plenary] meetings of the chambers. [The sessions of the Council of the Union and the Council of Nationalities begin and end at the same time.]

Article 113 [Article 111].—*The right of* legislative initiative in the USSR Supreme Soviet belongs to the Council of the Union, the Council of Nationalities, the Presidium of the USSR Supreme Soviet, the USSR Council of Ministers, the Union republics through their supreme bodies of state power, the committees of the USSR Supreme Soviet and the standing committees of its chambers, Deputies to the USSR Supreme Soviet, the USSR Supreme Court and the USSR Prosecutor General.

The right of legislative initiative also belongs to [mass] public organizations through their all-Union agencies.

Article 114 [Article 112].—*Draft laws and other questions submitted for consideration by the USSR Supreme Soviet are discussed by the chambers in separate or joint meetings. When necessary, a draft law or other question may be referred to one or more committees for preliminary or* *additional consideration.*[5]

A USSR law is considered adopted if each chamber of the USSR Supreme Soviet has passed it by majority vote of the total number of Deputies in the chamber. *Resolutions and other acts of the USSR Supreme Soviet are adopted by a majority of the total number of Deputies to the USSR Supreme Soviet.*

By a decision of the USSR Supreme Soviet or the Presidium of the USSR Supreme Soviet, adopted at their initiative or on a proposal by a Union republic, draft [USSR] laws *and other very important questions of state life* may be submitted for nationwide discussion [and also for nationwide vote (referendum)].

Article 115 [Article 113].—In the event of disagreement between the Council of the Union and the Council of Nationalities, the question is referred for settlement to a conciliation committee, formed by the chambers on a parity basis, after which the question is considered a second time by the Council of the Union and the Council of Nationalities at a joint meeting. *If agreement is again not reached, the question is held over for discussion by the next session of the USSR Supreme Soviet or is submitted by the Supreme Soviet for nationwide vote (referendum).*

Article 116 [Article 114].—USSR laws, resolutions and other acts of the USSR Supreme Soviet are published in the languages of the Union republics, over the signature of the Chairman and the Secretary of the Presidium of the USSR Supreme Soviet.

Article 117 [Article 115].—A Deputy to the USSR Supreme Soviet has the right to address inquiries to the USSR Council of Ministers, to ministers and to heads of other agencies formed by the USSR Supreme Soviet. The

USSR Council of Ministers or the official to whom the inquiry was addressed is obliged to provide an oral or written reply to the *particular* session of the USSR Supreme Soviet within three days.

Article 118 [Article 116].—A Deputy to the USSR Supreme Soviet may not have criminal proceedings instituted against him, be arrested or be subjected to an administrative penalty by court order without the consent of the USSR Supreme Soviet or, in intervals between its sessions, without the consent of the Presidium of the USSR Supreme Soviet.

Article 119 [Article 117].—The USSR Supreme Soviet elects, at a joint meeting of its chambers, the Presidium of the USSR Supreme Soviet — the continuously functioning agency of the USSR Supreme Soviet, accountable to the latter for all its activity *and exercising, within the limits stipulated by the Constitution, the functions of supreme body of state power of the USSR in intervals between sessions of the Supreme Soviet.*

Article 120 [Article 118].—The Presidium of the USSR Supreme Soviet is elected from among the Deputies and consists of the Chairman of the Presidium of the Supreme Soviet, the First Vice-Chairman, 15 Vice-Chairmen — one from each Union republic — the Secretary of the Presidium and 21 members of the Presidium of the USSR Supreme Soviet.

Article 121 [Article 119].—The Presidium of the USSR Supreme Soviet:

(1) *sets the dates for elections to the USSR Supreme Soviet;*

(2) [1 in the draft] convenes sessions of the USSR Supreme Soviet;

(3) [2] coordinates the activity of the standing committees of the chambers of the USSR Supreme Soviet;

(4) [3] exercises control over the observance of the USSR Constitution and ensures conformity between the Union-republic Constitutions *and laws* and the USSR Constitution *and laws;*

(5) [4] interprets USSR laws;

(6) [5] ratifies and abrogates international treaties of the USSR;

(7) [6] annuls resolutions and orders of the USSR Council of Ministers and the Union-republic Councils of Ministers if they do not conform to the law;

(8) [7] establishes military titles, diplomatic ranks and other special titles; confers the highest military titles, diplomatic ranks and other special titles;

(9) [8] institutes USSR orders and medals; establishes USSR titles of honor; awards USSR orders and medals; confers USSR titles of honor;

(10) [9] admits persons to USSR citizenship; resolves questions of the renunciation of USSR citizenship and the deprivation of USSR citizenship and questions of granting asylum;

(11) [10] issues all-Union acts of amnesty and exercises the right of pardon;

(12) [11] appoints and recalls *diplomatic* [plenipotentiary] representatives of the USSR to foreign states and international organizations;

(13) [12] accepts credentials and letters of recall of foreign states' diplomatic representatives accredited to it;

(14) [13] forms the USSR Defense Council and ratifies its composition, and appoints and removes the supreme command of the USSR Armed Forces;

(15) [14] in the interests of the USSR's defense, proclaims martial law in individual localities or throughout the country;

(16) [15] proclaims general or partial mobilization;

(17) [16] in intervals between sessions of the USSR Supreme Soviet, proclaims a state of war in the event of an armed attack on the USSR or when necessary to fulfill international treaty commitments providing for mutual defense against aggression;

(18) exercises other powers established by the USSR Constitution and laws.

Article 122 [Article 120].—In intervals between sessions of the Supreme Soviet, and with subsequent presentation for ratification at the next session, the Presidium of the USSR Supreme Soviet:

(1) when necessary, amends USSR *legislative acts* [legislation] currently in force;

(2) ratifies changes in the boundaries between Union republics;

(3) on proposals by the USSR Council of Ministers, forms and abolishes USSR ministries and USSR state committees;

(4) on representations from the Chairman of the USSR Council of Ministers, removes and appoints individual members of the USSR Council of Ministers.

Article 123 [Article 121].—The Presidium of the USSR Supreme Soviet issues decrees and adopts resolutions.

Article 124 [Article 122].—When the term of office of the USSR Supreme Soviet expires, the Presidium of the USSR Supreme Soviet retains its powers until the formation of a new Presidium by the newly elected USSR Supreme Soviet.

The newly elected USSR Supreme Soviet is convened by

the Presidium of the outgoing USSR Supreme Soviet no later than two months after the elections.

Article 125 [Article 123].—The Council of the Union and the Council of Nationalities elect from among the Deputies standing committees for the preliminary consideration and preparation of questions within the jurisdiction of the USSR Supreme Soviet, as well as for assistance in implementing USSR laws and other decisions of the USSR Supreme Soviet and its Presidium and for the exercise of control over the activity of state agencies and organizations. The chambers of the USSR Supreme Soviet may *also* create joint committees on a parity basis.

The USSR Supreme Soviet creates, when it considers it necessary, investigative, inspection and other committees on any question.[6]

All state *and public* agencies, *organizations* [institutions] and officials are obliged to fulfill the requirements of *the* [these] committees *of the USSR Supreme Soviet and the committees of its chambers* and to submit the necessary materials and documents to them.[6]

The committees' recommendations are subject to mandatory consideration by state and public agencies, institutions and organizations. Reports are to be made to the committees, within established time periods, on the results of such consideration or on the measures taken.

Article 126 [Article 124].—The USSR Supreme Soviet exercises control over the activity of all state agencies accountable to it.

The USSR Supreme Soviet forms a USSR People's Control Committee, which heads the system of people's control agencies.

The organization of and procedure for the activity of the

people's control agencies are defined by the Law on People's Control in the USSR.

Article 127 [Article 126].—The procedure for the activity of the USSR Supreme Soviet and its agencies is defined by the Regulations of the USSR Supreme Soviet and by *other* USSR laws issued on the basis of the USSR Constitution.

Chapter 16.
THE USSR COUNCIL OF MINISTERS.

Article 128 [Article 127].—The USSR Council of Ministers — the USSR government — is the supreme executive and administrative body of state power in the USSR.

Article 129 [Article 128].—The USSR Council of Ministers is formed by the USSR Supreme Soviet at a joint meeting of the Council of the Union and the Council of Nationalities and consists of the Chairman of the USSR Council of Ministers, the First Vice-Chairmen and Vice-Chairmen [of the USSR Council of Ministers], the USSR ministers and the chairmen of USSR state committees.

The Chairmen of the Union-republic Councils of Ministers are ex-officio members of the USSR Council of Ministers.

On a representation by the Chairman of the USSR Council of Ministers, the USSR Supreme Soviet may include the heads of other USSR agencies and organizations in the USSR government.

The USSR Council of Ministers tenders its resignation to a newly elected USSR Supreme Soviet at its first session.

Article 130 [Article 129].—The USSR Council of Ministers is responsible and accountable to the USSR Supreme Soviet, and, in intervals between sessions of the

USSR Supreme Soviet, to the Presidium of the USSR Supreme Soviet.

The USSR Council of Ministers makes regular reports on its work to the USSR Supreme Soviet.

Article 131 [Article 130].—The USSR Council of Ministers is empowered to resolve all questions of state administration within the jurisdiction of the USSR, insofar as they do not, *according to* [by force of] the Constitution, come within the purview of the USSR Supreme Soviet and the Presidium of the USSR Supreme Soviet.

Within the limits of its authority, the USSR Council of Ministers:

(1) ensures the guidance of the national economy and of social and cultural construction [and the implementation of a uniform policy in the field of science and technology]; works out and implements measures to ensure a rise in the people's well-being and their cultural level, *to develop science and technology and the rational utilization and conservation of natural resources,* to strengthen the [uniform] monetary and credit system, to conduct a uniform price, *pay and social security* policy, to organize state insurance and a uniform system of record-keeping and statistics; organizes the administration of industrial, construction and agricultural enterprises and associations, transportation and communication enterprises, banks and other organizations and institutions of Union subordination;

(2) works out and submits to the USSR Supreme Soviet current and long-range state plans for the *economic and social* development of the USSR [development of the national economy and for social and cultural construction in the USSR] and the USSR State Budget; takes steps to implement state plans and the budget; presents reports to the USSR Supreme Soviet on fulfillment of plans and the

budget;

(3) carries out measures to protect the interests of the state, to safeguard socialist property and public order and to ensure and protect the rights *and liberties* of citizens;

(4) takes steps to safeguard state security;

(5) exercises general guidance of the development of the USSR Armed Forces and determines the annual contingents of citizens subject to call-up for active military service;

(6) exercises general guidance in the field of relations with foreign states, foreign trade and economic, scientific, technical and cultural cooperation between the USSR and foreign countries; takes steps to ensure the fulfillment of the USSR's international treaties; ratifies and abrogates intergovernmental international treaties;

(7) when necessary, forms committees, chief administrations and other departments under the USSR Council of Ministers to deal with matters of economic, social, cultural and defense construction.[7]

Article 132 [Article 131].—The Presidium of the USSR Council of Ministers, consisting of the Chairman of the USSR Council of Ministers and the First Vice-Chairmen and Vice-Chairmen [of the USSR Council of Ministers], functions as a permanent agency of the USSR Council of Ministers to resolve questions related to ensuring the guidance of the national economy and other questions of state administration.

Article 133 [Article 132].—On the basis of and in fulfillment of USSR laws and *other decisions* [decrees] of the [Presidium of the] USSR Supreme Soviet *and its Presidium,* the USSR Council of Ministers issues resolutions and orders and verifies their execution. The execution of resolutions and orders of the USSR Council of Ministers is mandatory throughout the USSR.

Article 134 [Article 133].—On questions within USSR jurisdiction, the USSR Council of Ministers has the right to suspend *the execution of* resolutions and orders of the Union-republic Councils of Ministers and to annul acts of USSR ministries, USSR state committees and other agencies under its jurisdiction.

Article 135 [Article 134].—The USSR Council of Ministers coordinates and directs the work of the USSR all-Union and Union-republic ministries and state committees and other agencies under its jurisdiction.

The USSR all-Union ministries and state committees guide the branches of administration assigned to them *or exercise interbranch administration* throughout the USSR, directly or through agencies created by them.

The USSR Union-republic ministries and state committees guide the branches of administration assigned to them *or exercise interbranch administration,* as a rule, through the respective Union-republic ministries, state committees *and other agencies,* and directly administer *individual* enterprises and associations *of Union subordination* [on a list approved by the Presidium of the USSR Supreme Soviet]. *The procedure for transferring enterprises and associations from republic and local subordination to Union subordination is defined by the Presidium of the USSR Supreme Soviet.*

The USSR ministries and state committees are responsible for the state and development of the *spheres* [branches] of administration assigned to them; within the limits of their jurisdiction, issue acts on the basis of and in fulfillment of USSR laws, *other decisions* [decrees] of the [Presidium of the] USSR Supreme Soviet *and its Presidium,* and resolutions and orders of the USSR Council of Ministers; and organize and verify the execution of such acts.

Article 136 [Article 135].—The jurisdiction of the USSR Council of Ministers and its Presidium, the procedure for their activity, the [USSR] Council of Ministers' relations with *other state agencies* [the USSR ministries and USSR state committees], as well as the list of USSR all-Union and Union-republic ministries and state committees, are defined, *on the basis of the Constitution,* by the Law on the USSR Council of Ministers.

VI. PRINCIPLES OF THE STRUCTURE OF BODIES OF STATE POWER AND ADMINISTRATION IN THE UNION REPUBLICS.

Chapter 17.
THE SUPREME BODIES OF STATE POWER AND ADMINISTRATION IN THE UNION REPUBLIC.

Article 137 [Article 136].—The Union-republic Supreme Soviet is the supreme body of state power in the Union republic.

The Union-republic Supreme Soviet is empowered to resolve all questions placed in the jurisdiction of the Union republic by the USSR Constitution and the Union-republic Constitution.

The adoption of the Union-republic Constitution and its amendment; the ratification of state plans *for economic and social development* [the development of the economy and for social and cultural construction], of the Union-republic state budget *and of reports on their fulfillment;* and the formation of agencies accountable to the Union-republic Supreme Soviet are exercised exclusively by that body.

Union-republic laws are adopted [solely] by the Union-republic Supreme Soviet *or by popular vote (referendum) conducted by decision of the Union-republic Supreme Soviet.*

Article 138 [Article 137].—The Union-republic Supreme Soviet elects a Presidium of the Supreme Soviet — a continuously functioning agency of the Union-republic Supreme Soviet that is accountable to the latter for all its activity. The composition and powers of the Presidium of the Union-republic Supreme Soviet are defined by the Union-republic Constitution.

Article 139 [Article 138].—The Union-republic Supreme Soviet forms a Union-republic Council of Ministers — the Union-republic government — which is the supreme executive and administrative body of state power in the Union republic.

The Union-republic Council of Ministers is responsible and accountable to the Union-republic Supreme Soviet, and, in intervals between sessions of the Supreme Soviet, to the Presidium of the Union-republic Supreme Soviet.

Article 140 [Article 139].—The Union-republic Council of Ministers issues resolutions and orders on the basis of and in fulfillment of USSR and Union-republic *legislative acts* [laws] and of resolutions and orders of the USSR Council of Ministers, and organizes and verifies their execution.

Article 141 [Article 140].—The Union-republic Council of Ministers has the right to suspend *the execution of* resolutions and orders of autonomous-republic Councils of Ministers and to annul decisions and orders of the executive committees of territory, province and city (in cities of republic subordination) Soviets of People's Deputies, of autonomous-province Soviets of People's Deputies and, in Union republics not divided into provinces, of the executive committees of district and city Soviets of People's Deputies.

Article 142 [Article 141].—The Union-republic Council of Ministers coordinates and directs the work of the Union republic's Union-republic and republic ministries and state committees *and of other agencies under its jurisdiction.*

The Union republic's Union-republic ministries and state committees guide the branches of administration assigned to them *or exercise interbranch administration* and are subordinate both to the Union-republic Council of Ministers and to the appropriate USSR Union-republic ministry or USSR state committee.

The republic ministries and state committees guide the branches of administration assigned to them *or exercise interbranch administration* and are subordinate to the Union-republic Council of Ministers.

Chapter 18.
THE SUPREME BODIES OF STATE POWER AND ADMINISTRATION IN THE AUTONOMOUS REPUBLICS.

Article 143 [Article 142].—The autonomous-republic Supreme Soviet is the supreme body of state power in the autonomous republic.

The adoption of the autonomous-republic Constitution and its amendment; the ratification of state plans for *economic and social development* [the development of the economy and for social and cultural construction] and of the autonomous-republic state budget; and the formation of agencies accountable to the autonomous-republic Supreme Soviet are exercised exclusively by that body.

Autonomous-republic laws are adopted [solely] by the autonomous-republic Supreme Soviet.

Article 144 [Article 143].—The autonomous-republic Supreme Soviet elects the Presidium of the autonomous-republic Supreme Soviet and forms the autonomous-republic Council of Ministers — the autonomous-republic government.

Chapter 19.
LOCAL BODIES OF STATE POWER AND ADMINISTRATION.

Article 145 [Article 144].—The appropriate Soviets of People's Deputies are the bodies of state power in territories, provinces, autonomous provinces, autonomous regions, districts, cities, boroughs, settlements and rural communities.

Article 146 [Article 145].—The local Soviets of People's Deputies resolve all questions of local importance, proceeding from the general interests of the state and the interests of the citizens residing on the Soviet's territory, carry out decisions of higher state bodies, *guide the activity of lower-level Soviets of People's Deputies,* participate in the discussion of questions of republic and all-Union importance and submit proposals on them.

The *local* Soviets of People's Deputies, on their territory, guide state, economic, social and cultural construction; ratify plans for economic and social [and cultural] development and the local budget; exercise guidance over [the activity of] state agencies, enterprises, institutions and organizations under their jurisdiction; ensure the observance of laws and the protection of state and public order and the rights of citizens; and help to strengthen the country's defense capability.

Article 147 [Article 146].—Within the limits of their authority, the local Soviets of People's Deputies *ensure comprehensive economic and social development on their territory;* exercise control over the observance of legislation by enterprises, institutions and organizations of higher subordination located on the Soviets' territory; and coordinate and control these entities' activity in the fields of land use, conservation, construction, *the use of labor resources,* the production of consumer goods and the provision of social, cultural, consumer and other services to the population.

Article 148 [Article 147].—The local Soviets of People's Deputies adopt decisions within the limits of the *powers* [rights] granted them by USSR and Union- and autonomous-republic *legislation* [laws]. The execution of the decisions of local Soviets is mandatory for all enterprises, institutions and organizations located on the Soviet's territory, as well as for officials and citizens.

Article 149 [Article 148].—The executive and administrative agencies of the local Soviets of People's Deputies are executive committees elected by the Soviets from among their Deputies.

The executive committees report to the Soviets that elected them at least once a year, *as well as to meetings of labor collectives and of citizens at their places of residence.*

Article 150 [Article 149].—The executive committees of local Soviets of People's Deputies are directly accountable to both the Soviet that elected them and to higher executive and administrative bodies.

VII. JUSTICE, ARBITRATION AND PROSECUTOR'S SUPERVISION.

Chapter 20.
THE COURTS AND ARBITRATION.

Article 151 [Article 150].—In the USSR, justice is administered solely by the courts.

In the USSR there are the USSR Supreme Court, the Union-republic Supreme Courts, the autonomous-republic Supreme Courts, territory, province and city courts, autonomous-province courts, autonomous-region courts, district (city) people's courts, and the military tribunals in the Armed Forces.

Article 152 [Article 151].—All courts in the USSR are formed on the principle that the posts of judges and people's assessors are elective.

The people's judges of district (city) people's courts are elected by the citizens of the district (city) on the basis of universal, equal and direct suffrage by secret ballot for a term of five years. The people's assessors of district (city) people's courts are elected by meetings of *citizens* [working people] at places of work or residence by open ballot for a term of two and a half years.

Higher courts are elected by the appropriate Soviets of People's Deputies for a term of five years.

The judges of military tribunals are elected by the Presidium of the USSR Supreme Soviet for a term of five years, and people's assessors are elected by meetings of service-men for a term of two and a half years.

Judges and people's assessors are responsible to the voters or the agencies that elected them, *report to them, and may be recalled by them according to a procedure established by law* [and are accountable to them].

Article 153 [Article 152].—The USSR Supreme Court is the supreme judicial body of the USSR and exercises super-vision over the judicial activity of USSR courts, as well as of Union-republic courts, within the limits established by law.

The USSR Supreme Court is elected by the USSR Supreme Soviet [for a term of five years] and is composed of a chairman, vice-chairmen, members and people's assessors. The chairmen of the Union-republic Supreme Courts are ex-officio members of the USSR Supreme Court.

The organization of and procedure for the activity of the USSR Supreme Court are defined by the Law on the USSR Supreme Court.

Article 154 [Article 153].—The consideration of civil and criminal cases in all courts is done collegially; in courts of the first instance, it is done with the participation of people's assessors. In the administration of justice, people's assessors have all the rights of a judge.

Article 155 [Article 154].—Judges and people's assessors are independent and subordinate only to the law.

Article 156 [Article 155].—Justice in the USSR is admin-istered on the principle of the equality of citizens before the law and the court.

Article 157 [Article 156].—The examination of cases in all courts is open. The hearing of cases in closed court is permitted only in cases established by law and with the observance of all the rules of judicial procedure.

Article 158 [Article 157].—The defendant is guaranteed the right to defense.

Article 159 [Article 158].—Judicial proceedings are conducted in the language of the Union or autonomous republic, autonomous province or autonomous region, or in the language of the majority of the population of the given locality. Persons participating in the case who do not know the language in which the proceedings are conducted are ensured the right to become completely familiar with the materials of the case, to participate in the proceedings through an interpreter, and to address the court in their native language.

Article 160 [Article 159].—No one can be adjudged guilty of committing a crime and subjected to criminal punishment other than by the verdict of a court and in accordance with [criminal] law.

Article 161 [Article 160].—There are panels of lawyers to provide legal assistance to citizens and organizations. In cases stipulated by *legislation* [law], legal assistance to citizens is provided free of charge.

The organization of and procedure for the activity of the bar are defined by USSR and Union-republic legislation.

Article 162 [Article 161].—Representatives of public organizations and labor collectives are permitted to participate in court proceedings in civil and criminal cases.

Article 163 [Article 162].—The settlement of economic disputes between enterprises, institutions and organizations is carried out by state arbitration agencies, *within the limits of their jurisdiction.*

The organization of and procedure for the activity of state arbitration agencies are defined by *the Law on State Arbitration in the USSR* [law]. [Guidance of and supervision over the activity of all arbitration agencies is exercised by the USSR State Court of Arbitration. The Chief Arbiter of the USSR State Court of Arbitration is appointed by the USSR Supreme Soviet for a term of five years.]

Chapter 21.
THE PROSECUTOR'S OFFICE.

Article 164 [Article 163].—Supreme supervision over the precise and uniform execution of laws by all ministries, state committees and departments, enterprises, institutions and organizations, executive and administrative agencies of local Soviets of People's Deputies, collective farms, cooperative and other public organizations, officials and citizens is vested in the USSR Prosecutor General and in prosecutors subordinate to him.

Article 165 [Article 164].—The USSR Prosecutor General is appointed by the USSR Supreme Soviet, is responsible and accountable to it and, in intervals between sessions of the Supreme Soviet, to the Presidium of the USSR Supreme Soviet.

Article 166 [Article 165].—The prosecutors of Union republics, autonomous republics, territories, provinces and autonomous provinces are appointed by the USSR Prosecutor General. The prosecutors of autonomous regions and district and city prosecutors are appointed by the Union-republic prosecutors and approved by the USSR Prosecutor General.

Article 167 [Article 166].—The term of office of the USSR Prosecutor General and of all lower-ranking prosecutors is five years.

Article 168 [Article 167].—The agencies of prosecutor's offices exercise their powers independently of all local agencies and are subordinate solely to the USSR Prosecutor General.

The organization of and procedure for the activity of the agencies of *prosecutor's offices* [the USSR Prosecutor's Office] are defined by the Law on *the USSR Prosecutor's Office* [Prosecutor's Supervision in the USSR].

VIII. THE EMBLEM, FLAG, ANTHEM AND CAPITAL OF THE USSR.

Article 169 [Article 168].—The State Emblem of the Union of Soviet Socialist Republics is a depiction of a hammer and sickle against the background of a globe, shown in the rays of the sun and framed by ears of grain, with the inscription "Proletarians of All Countries, Unite!" in the languages of the Union republics. There is a five-pointed star *in the upper part of* [above] the emblem.

Article 170 [Article 169].—The State Flag of the Union of Soviet Socialist Republics is a rectangular red cloth with a depiction in its upper corner, near the staff, of a gold hammer and sickle and above this a red five-pointed star, edged in gold. The ratio of the flag's width to its length is 1:2.

Article 171 [Article 170].—The National Anthem of the Union of Soviet Socialist Republics is approved by the Presidium of the USSR Supreme Soviet.

Article 172 [Article 171].—The city of Moscow is the capital of the Union of Soviet Socialist Republics.

IX. THE LEGAL EFFECT OF THE USSR CONSTITUTION AND THE PROCEDURE FOR AMENDING IT.[8]

Article 173 [Article 172].—The USSR Constitution has supreme legal force. All laws and other acts of state agencies are issued on the basis of and in conformity with the USSR Constitution. [The USSR Constitution goes into effect at the time it is adopted.]

Article 174 [Article 173].—The USSR Constitution is changed by a decision of the USSR Supreme Soviet, adopted by a majority of at least two-thirds of the total number of Deputies in each of its chambers.

Footnotes

1. [proclaim their aims and principles, establish the foundations for the organization of the socialist state of all the people, and formalize them in this Constitution]

2. Article 8 expands on Article 16 of the draft (dropped in the final text), which read: [Collectives of working people and public organizations participate in the management of enterprises and associations, in the resolution of questions of the organization of labor and everyday life and of the use of funds earmarked for the development of production and for social and cultural needs and material incentives.]

3. This paragraph replaces the third paragraph of Article 11 of the draft: [The property of trade union and other public organizations is the property they need to carry out their statutory tasks.]

4. [USSR citizens elect and may be elected to Soviets of People's Deputies, and they participate in the discussion and elaboration of draft laws and decisions of nationwide and local importance, in the work of state agencies and of cooperative and other public organizations, in exercising control over their activity, in the management of production and the affairs of labor collectives, and in meetings at places of residence.]

5. [After a draft law has been discussed at meetings of the chambers, it may be referred for consideration to one or more committees. The chambers also have the right to discuss and vote on a draft law without

referring it to a committee. USSR laws, resolutions and other acts of the USSR Supreme Soviet are adopted at separate or joint meetings of the chambers.]

6. In the draft, these two paragraphs constitute Article 125.

7. In the draft, this section is the second paragraph of Article 131.

8. In the draft, this head reads: PROCEDURE FOR PUTTING THE USSR CONSTITUTION INTO EFFECT AND AMENDING IT.

Textbooks on Soviet Politics

Armstrong, John A. *Ideology, Politics, and Government in the Soviet Union.* 4th ed. 1978. Praeger/Holt Rinehart & Winston.

Aspaturian, Vernon V. "The Soviet Union," in *Modern Political Systems: Europe.* Roy C. Macridis and Robert E. Ward, eds. 4th ed. 1978. Prentice-Hall.

Barghoorn, Frederick C. *Politics in the U.S.S.R.* 2nd ed. 1972. Little Brown.

Barry, Donald D. and Carol Barner Barry. *Contemporary Soviet Politics: An Introduction.* 1978. Prentice-Hall.

Carter, Gwendolen M. *Government of the Soviet Union.* 3rd ed. 1972. Harcourt Brace Jovanovich.

Churchward, L.G. *Contemporary Soviet Government.* 2nd ed. 1975. Elsevier.

Fainsod, Merle. *How Russia Is Ruled.* rev. ed. 1963. Harvard University Press. [Fainsod, Merle and Jerry F. Hough, 3rd ed., forthcoming.]

Hammer, Darrell P. *U.S.S.R. The Politics of Oligarchy.* 1974. Holt, Rinehart & Winston.

Hazard, John N. *Soviet System of Government.* 4th ed. 1968. University of Chicago Press. [5th ed., forthcoming.]

Laird, Roy D. *The Soviet Paradigm.* 1970. Free Press.

Lane, David. *Politics and Society in the USSR.* 1971. Random House.

McAuley, Mary. *Politics and the Soviet Union.* 1977. Penguin.

Osborn, Robert J. *The Evolution of Soviet Politics.* 1974. Dorsey Press.

Raymond, Ellsworth. *The Soviet State.* 2nd ed. 1977. New York University Press.

Reshetar, John S. *Soviet Polity: Government and Politics in the U.S.S.R.* 1971. Dodd Mead.

Rothman, Stanley and George W. Breslauer. *Soviet Politics and Society.* 1977. West Publishing Co.

Schapiro, Leonard. *Government and Politics in the Soviet Union.* rev. ed. 1978. Random House.

Wesson, Robert G. *The Soviet State: An Aging Revolution.* 1972. Wiley.

ROBERT WHALEN